No longer the property of the
Boston Public Library.
Sale of this material benefits the Library

JUST AN ORDINARY WOMAN BREATHING

21ST CENTURY ESSAYS

David Lazar and Patrick Madden, Series Editors

JUST AN ORDINARY WOMAN BREATHING

Julie Marie Wade

MAD CREEK BOOKS, AN IMPRINT OF
THE OHIO STATE UNIVERSITY PRESS
COLUMBUS

Copyright © 2020 by The Ohio State University.
All rights reserved.
Mad Creek Books, an imprint of The Ohio State University Press.

Library of Congress Cataloging-in-Publication Data
Names: Wade, Julie Marie, author.
Title: Just an ordinary woman breathing / Julie Marie Wade.
Other titles: 21st century essays.
Description: Columbus : Mad Creek Books, an imprint of The Ohio State University Press, [2020] | Series: 21st century essays | Summary: "Follows the author's progression of a personal education in embodiment, gender, sexuality, and love, where education includes both formal schooling and experiential encounters with familial, religious, and sociocultural expectations for what a woman's body should be and should do, and who a woman's body is for"—Provided by publisher.
Identifiers: LCCN 2019035553 | ISBN 9780814255674 (paperback) | ISBN 0814255671 (paperback) | ISBN 9780814277607 (ebook) | ISBN 0814277608 (ebook)
Subjects: LCSH: Wade, Julie Marie. | American essays—21st century.
Classification: LCC PS3623.A345 J87 2020 | DDC 818/.603—dc23
LC record available at https://lccn.loc.gov/2019035553

Cover design by Nathan Putens
Type set in Adobe Sabon

♾ The paper used in this publication meets the minimum requirements of the American National Standard for Information Sciences—Permanence of Paper for Printed Library Materials. ANSI Z39.48-1992.

For Angie
ever & always

CONTENTS

PART I

OVERTURE

Dangerous the epiphany that you are old enough to have a history. This is a danger like no other, except perhaps the danger of that primeval epiphany: You have a body. *Have? Are?* No one is sure, not even Descartes, but he will serve as whipping boy for all our accusations of embodiment. Bodies severed from the slip-knot of consciousness. Scarecrow bodies. Tin Man bodies. Bodies scrutinized by their self-same bodies. Bodies sending chain letters to themselves. Hyperactive bodies. Catatonic bodies. Bodies with feet in ruby shoes. Bodies that rest while their minds wander. Minds that rest while their bodies wander. (Somnambulist bodies are among the most compelling bodies.) Dreaming bodies. Dying bodies. Bodies remodeled like eat-in kitchens. Bodies refurbished like easy chairs. Somehow, we suspect, Descartes had a hand in it—hand or mind. *Do I think therefore I am, or am I therefore I think?* This is not unlike the Prince's question to Cinderella at the ball: *Do I love you because you're beautiful, or are you beautiful because I love you?* The idea of a beautiful body. The idea of a not-so-beautiful body. Other ideas apart from the body but in which the body is implicated, charged: Anonymous sex. Astral projection. DNA testing. Test-tube conception. Fingerprints lifted from a glass. A face dissolving in a photograph—when faces were still captured on film. The astronaut with her tether, beyond gravity now: nothing but a fleck in the darkness. The interstellar body is a stellar body indeed. Starlight: sweet heavenly body.

⧗

You have a history, and a body. You are a history, and a body. Your body has (is) a history, too.

There is a time for the evening under starlight,
A time for the evening under lamplight
(The evening with the photograph album)

You have a family, which is a constellation of bodies. The image of their bodies preserved in the photograph album. This is a hard truth for your small self to grasp: that you are *of* them; derivative, not duplicate; *flesh of their flesh, bone of their bone.* (No one claims *mind of their mind, soul of their soul.*) It is like the words you repeat in church, the words about Jesus who is *of* God, Jesus who is also part Father and part Ghost—though he is *triplicate,* like the white copy you keep, the pink copy you tear, the yellow you stow in the drawer.

Jesus, who is onion skin and white light and wafer. Jesus, who once had a body, was stripped of a body, transcended a body, only to float and swirl like ether above you. A hypothetical substance now, *disembodied,* imagined by ancients to occupy the upper regions of the sky. Ether Jesus. It is hard to picture him without his body, without his shepherd's clothes and tousled hair, his trim beard and surprisingly feminine features, which you have passed time admiring in the Sunday school portrait. Now Androgynous Jesus has been replaced by this colorless, highly volatile, flammable Jesus—*solvent, inhalant, anesthetic*—the one you are told to ask into your heart, the one you are told must reside there.

The members of your family are not beautiful the way Embodied Jesus is beautiful. Your grandmother, who has such a kind face, points to a picture of a woman with dark, tight curls. She says, "There I am. See? That was your grandmother"—tapping with her fingernail—"before she was even your grandmother. What do you think of that?"

I study the photograph, frightened. I see nothing that unites her past and present bodies. *How did she become someone else altogether? How did she lose all resemblance to herself?*

"Would you like to see your grandfather?" she asks. He has been dead a long time, longer than I have been alive. This is no barrier to love, I know, because he comes to me animate in stories, draws close to me in the ether of my dreams, watching over. Grandpa John—like a second beneficent Jesus—who was once made of the same stuff of which I am now made. His face in the photograph startles me. I love him, and yet he is not beautiful. *How can this be? How can my love not make him beautiful?* The wide-set eyes, the sallow cheeks, the lips set awkwardly over his teeth. There is nothing like Androgynous Jesus about him, nothing of the chiseled movie star jaw validated by my father, venerated by my mother.

"I thought he would look like Rock Hudson," I murmur.

Grandma laughs at me. "Why would he look like Rock Hudson, dear, when no one else in our family does?"

This is another hard truth: we are not a constellation of movie stars. The most beautiful among us is Aunt Linda, and I have heard my mother say it more than once—"Her beauty is beginning to fade"—like a photograph left out in the sun. This is just what happens. Beauty can't last. It was made to be *ephemeral,* a word I clasp like a locket, which I will open someday when I find the right picture to place inside. For now, I hear no distinction between *ephemeral* and *ethereal.* They are angel words. They are beyond the realm of human comprehension.

I ask my father, "Who is the most beautiful woman who has ever lived?" He tells me the answer is subjective, which means nothing yet—which means only that he is stalling. Finally:

"Grace Kelly. Princess Grace." I want to see her, and so we look together at the early scenes of a movie called *Rear Window.*

The man does not look like a movie star to me, which might explain why he is always hiding behind a camera. When he wakes, there is a woman bending over him. She is the way I picture Cinderella, and Sleeping Beauty, too. Though I have never seen her before, she is familiar. I want to know how it is I know she is beautiful, but this is given, the way the names of things are given. God asked Adam to write the dictionary. He put words to things, and he invented their synonyms and their antonyms, and it is my (first) great sadness in life that I was not asked, that I was not even consulted. I want to call out the names of things and make the things they are appear. Names—and their corollary bodies.

Grace Kelly is a synonym for beauty, the way that Princess is a synonym for beauty. In a picture dictionary, you would see BEAUTY and then the funny marks beside it—in case you couldn't count its syllables or make the necessary sounds—and then you would see Princess Grace with her dark red lips and the bright white pearls resting across the perfect symmetry of her collarbones. Even her name is beautiful, I muse, though GRACE, by definition, has two meanings. Adam's meaning is *poise, elegance,* like a princess or a ballerina or a lady movie star. It is unclear to me whether men can have grace or whether this word belongs to women only, like teacups and geraniums.

Many years after Adam, Jesus came, and he added another entry to the dictionary. Jesus always writes in red. Grace became *undeserved favor.* I have been granted this grace, but not the first grace, not the Grace Kelly grace—which is also Kim Novak grace and Eva Marie Saint grace, her name further showing her undeserved favor. I am not sure how I know, but I understand implicitly that I will not grow into a graceful woman. Thankfully, though, I will be saved by grace through faith alone.

(A small pondering: *If beauty is not required to receive God's grace, then why are angels always beautiful?*)

My grandmother was one of nine children. She had six brothers and two sisters. One is Great Aunt Ruth, who lives in Canada and smuggles fruits and chocolates under her hat when she comes to visit us in these United States. She is thin as a rod, as a flagpole, a flat body like a boy's body, even though she always wears a dress. Aunt Ruth is gentle and wise, and though to be thin I am learning is a kind of beauty, she is not graceful. Her hair on her head like a dollop of frosting. Her laugh that bursts forth, too big for her body.

When Ruth is here, the sisters drink coffee and play with cards. They reminisce about the old days, when everyone lived in Canada and their mother cooked with real fire. They take out the photograph albums, because memory is slippery like a fish on a line. There are fishes that have fallen back in the water.

"This was your Great Aunt Ethel," my grandmother says, sliding a photograph toward me.

"She's been gone such a long time," Ruth laments. "What was it—1924, 25?"

The picture is not quite black-and-white, not quite color. The woman's lips are bowed, her brows dark and arched, her hair blond, and her skin unblemished. She is pink and white in all the right places. She wears pearls that dip down into the soft flesh below her collarbones. "Was she a movie star?" I demand. "Did we have a movie star in our family?"

"Well, Ethel moved to New York City in the 1920s. She lived with Oscar, her husband, in a brownstone the way people do there. She wanted to be a dancer and a singer on Broadway."

"*Was she?*" I am holding my breath and only just discover it, gulping the air fast and sudden into my lungs.

They exchange knowing glances, the way grown-ups do. "She tried," my grandmother sighs. "She had a beautiful voice and a beautiful face. Perhaps if she had gone to Hollywood instead. Perhaps she could have found her place in the pictures.

As it was, though . . ." Her voice trails off, and they both sip their coffee in silence.

"What happened to Great Aunt Ethel?" I persist.

"She died young," Ruth says. "It was a tragic thing. Hers was a body for the sixties, not the twenties." Her long, slender fingers unwrap Hershey's kisses, one by one. The little balls of foil form an ellipsis out to the saucer's edge.

"I don't understand"—a phrase that spills from my lips like a song's relentless chorus. "What does that mean?"

My grandmother pats my hand. "It's strange the way standards of beauty change. In the twenties, it was the flapper look—thin girls without hips or chests—thin girls with bobbed hair and long beads."

I turn to Aunt Ruth and smile. "Were you a flapper?" She laughs like I have said the silliest thing, though a light blush crests over her cheeks.

"In the sixties, it was Marilyn Monroe. Your Aunt Ethel was built like that—the classic hourglass."

Now Marilyn Monroe I know. I have thought before how she is beautiful but sad in her beauty—different from the graceful blond movie stars who appear in Alfred Hitchcock's films. In Seaside each summer: her likeness imprinted on lunchboxes and wall clocks of the novelty shops, her face for sale in the galleries, framed or unframed, photographed or painted.

"Did she—did *Marilyn*—" her sadness makes me feel closer to her, like I don't have to use her last name—"die young?"

More knowing glances, and then my grandmother replies: "That's a story for another time."

My first diary is not a journal. My thoughts do not flow freely like a Hollywood starlet's hair gleaming in sun as some man drives her above the sea in a powder blue convertible. I like this image, but I cannot write the way this image feels. Instead, I make inventories the way a scientist would. I am becoming scientific in my studies of beauty and the body.

For instance, my mother has a scar on her left hand. This is not the hand she writes with; it is the hand where her wedding ring adorns her finger.

"What happened there?" I inquire.

We are kneeling in the soft earth of our garden. My mother has taken off her gloves and rests a moment on her heels, which is rare. My mother's body is a body in motion, like a cosmic body, her heart a frantic comet that orbits the earth and sometimes, without warning, veers off-course, plunging toward the sun. Comets, I later learn, have been observed by thinkers since ancient times and have traditionally been considered bad omens.

"I don't remember," my mother says, her hand limp as a fish against her thigh, the scar a dark crescent rising over her knuckle. "It was probably a kitchen knife, but it could have been a trowel like this one." We regard the trowel a moment, its steel spider legs wedged into the soil.

"Will it go away?" I want to know. This is important, bordering on urgent. "How long will it take to go away?"

"Oh, I doubt it ever will," she replies. Her tone is casual, indifferent. "It might fade some more over time, but that's as much as this cut is ever going to heal."

Her knees snap as she rises to standing.

"But—"

My mother turns to me, perplexed. "But what?"

"Doesn't it make you sad?" My heart a minor planet still, but spinning, spinning, fast as a plate on a magician's stick.

"Of course not. Why should it? It's not like the scar is on my face."

Memo: My mother's hands are not beautiful. This strikes me as a tragic thing. It seems like a mother's hands <u>should</u> be beautiful, small and smooth. But her fingers are large and wrinkled at the joints, and her palms are dry as sandpaper, as a paint swatch laid out on the kitchen counter. At first I thought it was only the scar. Then I realized, even without the scar, her hands <u>still</u> wouldn't be beautiful.

⧗

There's a hierarchy to beauty, I am learning. At first, face takes precedence over other places. I sit at the wicker vanity in my bedroom, the lights dim, the record needle scratching against the last tune: *Send in the Clowns.* Cautiously, I peer into the mirror. My face is round, my skin is tan, my lips are cracked from where I bite them and they bleed. My eyes are big and blue, but one is larger than the other. This is because only one is good for seeing while the other serves mostly as decoration. My hair is brown and shoulder-length and curly with home permanent. My mother has mentioned before that my eyelashes are too short for a girl and says she looks forward to the day when I can start wearing mascara.

It is hard to know what to say about my face, let alone what to write in my notations. If I were beautiful, I think I would have discovered so by now—would have felt the beauty coming into me like a magical power. *As yet, I couldn't levitate. As yet, I couldn't turn myself into a cloud.* And if I were ugly, I assume I would have been told so, too.

With my glasses on, of course, I am ugly. I have learned this much, but glasses are easy to remove. The lawyers on television would call them *circumstantial,* which means inadmissible as evidence. My glasses could not be slipped into a Ziploc bag and assigned a number in the court. My glasses could not be referenced as proof of ugliness. Yet it is my (second) great sadness in life that perhaps I have no features that distinguish me at all. If it cannot be stated conclusively that I am beautiful or ugly—what am I? *Ordinary? Inconsequential?* I hear a gavel in these words. Am I that treacherous phrase my mother has been known to mutter?

"Grandma, do you think I'm a *Plain Jane?*" I stand beside the table where she plays Solitaire.

"Of course not, dear. You're a perfectly lovely Julie. Whatever gave you that idea?"

"I don't know. Except—there doesn't seem to be anything special about my face."

She lays down her cards and presses the pad of her finger to the top of my lip. "Right there. What about that? I'd say that's a bona fide beauty mark."

Memo: Grandma says the black freckle under my nose is actually a beauty mark. Many beautiful women have had them, including the supermodel Cindy Crawford and even the movie star Marilyn Monroe. Grandma says a long time ago women who wanted to appear less ordinary (more beautiful?) applied false beauty marks to their faces. This was common in those times, the way I might wear a sticker on my hand at a carnival or have my cheeks painted by one of the clowns.

I notice my father never says much about bodies. At least, he never volunteers. But there is a *Sports Illustrated* calendar dangling from a pin on his wall and a picture book beside his desk called *Bathing Beauties*. I assume he finds these women beautiful, their bodies sleek and long, shimmery with water or lightly dusted with sand. Often, though, it is hard to make out their faces, and harder still to distinguish one smooth, smiling face from another.

My mother is taking so long putting on her makeup that we wander—slowly but deliberately—the two scant blocks from our motor lodge to the stunning Oregon shore. "I like that they call it a *body of water,*" I say, to break the ice that doesn't usually need breaking.

My father is quiet today because during the night, he has asked my mother to do something that she has refused to do. I heard in his hushed, urgent tones a version of my voice and sensed his own planet heart was spinning round too hard.

I wasn't sure what it was he wanted from her, but I knew married bodies were different somehow—the way the pastor said (and lingered on the words), "Now the two shall become one; the man shall cleave to his wife, and the wife shall cleave to her husband."

"What does *cleave* mean?" I ask my father. We spread our towels over the soft, packed sand, stretch out on our backs in the sun.

"That's a strange word," he says. "It means to bind together, but also to break apart."

"But—how is that possible? How can a word be its own antonym?" *That Adam. That rascal. How I hated him!*

My father isn't interested in language the way I am. Words are all function for him—like pointing a finger at something you want, a gesture made by the tongue. But for me they are form, they are sound, they are sacred somehow. They have colors and textures, even flavors sometimes, or a fragrance once in a while. Words, for me, are embodied, and like anything that has (is) a body, a word can be beautiful, or graceful, or ugly in a way that makes you wish you could close your ears.

One of the ugliest words I know is *stomach,* its taste and texture one and the same—the paste of unsalted crackers stuck to the roof of the mouth. *STUM-ick. STUM-ick.* There is no nice way to say it, and I am not pleased with any of its synonyms: *tummy, belly, abdomen, mid-section.* My father tugs his shirt over his head, the way all men do, and hands me the suntan lotion. "Have I told you about the time my father fell asleep on this beach?" He has, but I don't interrupt him. "He forgot his sunblock and was burned from his neck all the way to his toes. His stomach turned red as a lobster, and he couldn't drive his car for a week." This was before my grandmother had a license of her own, so the family was stranded at the shore. "It seems wrong to say," my father sighs, "but that was one of the happiest weeks of my life."

I kneel in the sand behind my father, rubbing the lotion over his shoulders and down the length of his spine. He loves reminiscing about his childhood—this beach, those waves. I love my father, so I listen. I study the map of his flesh, which is perhaps less of a map and more of a code in need of cracking: the deep creases in his pale skin, the small islands of black hair, the chaos of freckles that lack a shape and certain resolution. Less organized than ellipses, they appear as interpuncts, dotting his body's landscape like old-fashioned multiplication signs.

Then, my mother comes, and they lie side by side in the sun, not speaking or touching. My mother doesn't love the beach the way my father does. She would rather read her book or work her crossword page than gaze out past the pink and green umbrellas at the wild spectacle of the waves. Under her breath: "I'll never understand," she says, "how people can pass whole days like this," which means not only *I find the beach boring* but also *I want to hurt you very much, Bill,* and *I am hoping Julie will take after me.* This is the way language is like skin: there are layers to it, and eventually, no matter what you say, you are bound to strike blood or bone.

Memo: My father has a mangled toe from where, as a child, he stubbed it hard on a rock in the surf. My mother has purple fireworks that light up the flesh of her thighs. These, she says, are a consequence of giving birth. What happened to my father happened before I was born, so it is not my fault. But what happened to my mother is something I have caused—like her stomach that won't lay flat from where the muscles were stretched, the skin broken. She has shown me before, explained her sacrifice. It is my (third) great sadness in life that I have made my mother less beautiful just by being born.

⧗

A few times a year, we pack our bags and pile into the car and drive to a place outside the city called Black Diamond. It has not escaped my noticing that these words—*black* and *diamond*—when paired together form an oxymoron. They are like Romeo's *sweet sorrow.* I am also aware that the words correspond to a picture I have seen, marking treacherous ski slopes at Crystal Mountain. I am not yet experienced enough to take advanced runs indicated by the black diamond. So far only my mother and her sister Sharon can. But I am making progress. Just a year ago, I was following the green circles, and now, suddenly, I have found a new level of control. Even my teacher remarked I am becoming more coordinated and skillful in my movements. Now I belong with the blue squares that signal *intermediate.*

Here in Black Diamond, the paths are narrow, the visibility low. You never know what to expect when you turn a corner. My mother's parents live in one house; my mother's sister, her husband, and daughter live in the house next door. They are the mirror image of us—a tall father who tells jokes; an angry mother who compares herself to others; a lonely only child. Sometimes it is more like a funhouse mirror. My Uncle Thor is diabetic, which means his body has been known to deceive him. He carries candies that we aren't allowed to pilfer in his pockets and the glove box of his car. Once, he was driving when the thick insulin fog began to roll over him, but he was out of Lifesavers, which is ironic on its own. Thor turned into the 7-Eleven in search of a quick sugar fix, but he blacked out before he could put the car in park and barreled through the big glass windows.

The clerk assumed he was drunk. The bystanders continued to stand by and stare. When the medics came, Thor remembered everything that had happened. He knew Reagan in the White House, his birthday in May, but they couldn't release him until he remembered his wife's name. "We need her to come down here and get you," they said. He saw her face in his mind, all her features, but he couldn't, for the life of him, make his lips contort the right way.

My Aunt Sharon is hard to describe, but I don't see how you could forget her. She didn't like to dress up the way my mother did, or wear much makeup, or style her hair. I think she only cared about beauty vicariously—a story she wrote through her daughter. Sometimes for days on end, I saw her drink nothing but coffee and only from the thermos she carried. It was long with an industrial strap and a khaki green cup that doubled as the lid. She wore sweatshirts and jeans and big boots with deep treads. She walked hard like a soldier and was very fond of shaking her head.

"Your mother looks so different in these pictures," I say to my cousin Blythe. "You can still tell it's her, but everything about her demeanor has changed."

"*Demeanor?*" Blythe is a year younger, and her vocabulary is not as advanced as mine. In language, I have reached the double black diamond.

We sprawl on our grandmother's sewing room floor—without her permission—sorting through the pictures in her drawers. "It means the expression on her face and the way she holds herself. Basically, it's her attitude toward the world."

"This was their wedding picture," Blythe says, pointing to her parents when they were both young and blond, her father a full foot taller than her mother the way my father is, too. *It's literal and metaphorical,* I think to myself: *they have trouble seeing eye to eye.* "They got married in Reno, Nevada, which is a place where people go to gamble."

"Why didn't they have a big church wedding?" I ask, thinking of my mother's silky white gown, my father's glossy black tux, their altar of flowers.

"They wanted to elope," she boasts. "They wanted to do something daring."

"It's not that daring if you have time to take a picture." There is something smug about my cousin that I feel compelled to challenge. My mother would call it *putting her in her place.*

"When you're in love, you don't always plan ahead," Blythe tells me with an air of authority.

"Well, my mother says that *real love waits.*"

"What does that mean?" She calls my bluff with my own favorite question.

"To tell you the truth," I concede, "I'm not really sure." *Why would love wait, and for what?*

⧗

When our grandmother finds us alone with her things, she shouts about our disrespect and calls us trespassers. She says she knows she can't expect much of me because my father is a permissive parent. But Blythe, she says—*Blythe should know better.* Grandma Tena, whose name is spelled wrong on purpose, does not have such a kind face as my father's mother, but she is younger and stands straighter in her body and some would say, without knowing the whole story, that she is the more beautiful one.

Because my grandfather is silent in his chair, silent at the dinner table, and silent before the television screen, my grandmother does all the talking in their house, dispenses all the punishments. My mother and my aunt, in their own houses, also take the lead in these matters. My father, however, does not believe in physical penalties. He argues for time-outs and groundings. He thinks the mind should be chastised, not the body.

This is why I am left behind when my grandmother bends my cousin over the toilet seat with the fluffy pink cover, when my grandmother disciplines her with hand or hairbrush. "When we were children," my mother says, calm and without wincing, "she used to beat us with wooden spoons. After a while, she only had to rattle the kitchen drawer, and we would stop whatever it was we were doing."

When I hear a story like this, I want to wrap my arms around my mother's waist and press my head against the soft pillow of her stomach. Then, I remember how my father says, "If children are hit, they grow up scared, or mean, or both. They grow up knowing that nothing they have—nothing they *are*—is ever really their own." He isn't sure how to explain the body either. I stand by my mother in the carpeted kitchen, listening as my cousin wails. When I look over at her, I am suddenly taller. We stand at eye level now, but I am *growing like a weed* and will soon surpass her. It is the (fourth) great sadness of my life that my mother and I will never see eye to eye again.

Linda and Sharon have a younger brother, Steve. He was a pretty baby with golden curls and long gold lashes. Everyone thought he was a girl. When Steve got older, he cut his hair short and played fast-pitch baseball. Then, he hurt his shoulder and ended up the principal of an elementary school in a farm town called Chehalis. He married our Aunt Arlene and had a daughter, Erin. He became silent like his father and angry like his mother and grew a mustache and a round potbelly. But in childhood pictures, he resembles the cherubim. He could have been a Gerber baby.

(A small pondering: *Does a fall from beauty correspond to a fall from grace?*)

These are the relatives we seldom see, but I am intrigued by the idea that we are *related.* How can this be when we don't even know each other, when we are only distant names and indistinct faces in photographs? My father says we carry history in our genes, and scientists are working on a project to map those genes—a giant blueprint of all our human bodies. This is relevant—a word that reminds me of *relative*—because Uncle Steve and Aunt Arlene are having another baby. They have braided their genes together again, and in two months' time, we will receive the birth announcement of our youngest cousin, Lacie.

"When you have the baby," I ask Aunt Arlene, "will she have blond hair and blue eyes like Uncle Steve or dark hair and dark eyes like you and Erin?"

"Dark," she says with certainty.

"How do you know?" We sit on the floor with our legs spread wide like dance class, and Aunt Arlene's large belly rests between her thighs.

"It has to do with genes," she replies. "Certain genes are dominant, and others are recessive." I stare at her blankly. "In other words, certain traits are more likely to be expressed than others. Brown eyes, for instance, mask blue. Black hair masks blond."

"Always?"

"I think so. You'll find that, compared to all the people of the world, dark eyes and dark hair are much more common. Blond hair and blue eyes are comparatively rare."

Since Aunt Arlene is Japanese, I figure she has much more knowledge about the people of the world. After all, she has seen more of them. She is young for a grown-up but also wise, and beautiful in a different way than anyone else I know. Her hair is straight as a stick and shiny like polished shoes. She wears a headband the way you would in first grade.

"Do you want to feel the baby kick?" Before I can answer, she places my hand on the hump of her dress. I can tell her skin is stretched to nearly bursting now, and I am sorry a little thinking of how it will never be perfect again. We wait awhile, but the baby is still.

During this time, I study Aunt Arlene's face, trying to commit her to memory. After all, I may never see her again. She lives far away with Uncle Steve on the other side of the mountains, and my mother and her brother no longer speak, even when they stand in the same room.

"Is there a gene for beauty?" I whisper, not wanting the others to hear.

She laughs, and the water in her belly jostles. "It would have to be a lot of genes, I think. Beauty has so many different forms."

Memo: My parents promise I can be anything I want to be, but so much of <u>who</u> we are and <u>how</u> we are is predetermined.

I cannot, for instance, be a figure skater (like the women I love to watch in the Olympics) because I am not graceful and cannot balance on a single, silver blade. I have long, thin fingers, so they tell me to play piano. I am tall and sturdy in my frame, so they tell me to play basketball. But then Aunt Arlene says some genes mask other genes, and I think about those genes in hiding, the ones that are cramped and shy and too afraid to ever express themselves. I think about the ways my body has learned to operate in disguise.

For hours on the tennis court, Blythe and Erin and I take turns giving birth. We stuff sofa cushions under our shirts, lie down on our backs, and press the soles of our feet together. We breathe as hard as we can and scream and moan like Wally's wife on *The New Leave It to Beaver.* We writhe on the ground while the other cousins steady our knees, confer about the grim prognosis—women, we know, can die of childbirth—then drag the thick, scratchy cushion out.

"Your body is never the same after," I say. I am the oldest, which gives me a certain credibility. "You'll always be a little fatter than you were before and bashful about wearing your bathing suit in public."

But then Blythe, determined to trump everything I say, announces dramatically—"My mother didn't even *give birth.* I wasn't even actually *born.*"

Erin's jaw drops, and her head shakes like a bobble doll on the hood of a speeding car. "*What?*" The word seems to pour from her mouth in slow motion, like she is filling a pitcher with the sound of it.

"That's not even possible," I dismiss. "Don't you know anything about science?"

"No, it is! It *is!* You should see the scar on her stomach from where they had to stitch her back up."

Blythe claims our Aunt Sharon never lay on her back in a hospital bed, eating ice chips and pushing a baby through the nameless black diamond between her legs. She claims they knocked her mother out—like chloroform over the mouth in Hitchcock films—then sawed open her abdomen and lifted baby Blythe directly into the light.

"There must have been so much blood and guts," Erin murmurs, making the gross-out face. "You're lucky you can't remember it."

Unconvinced, I resolve to consult my encyclopedia before I weigh in on this matter.

At Blythe's house, we pile onto the sectional sofa in front of the big screen TV, the dogs like bookmarks between us and the VCR set to play *White Christmas*. Uncle Thor is in the kitchen making a sandwich. This is where he often stands in my memory, his body so long he is nothing but a pair of trousers when you look back at the pass-through window.

"It's February, you know," he calls to us. "Shouldn't you be watching something for Valentine's Day?"

"No, Dad!" Blythe shouts, fast-forwarding through the boring parts at the beginning. "And don't talk with your mouth full." Her voice sounds older than she is and suddenly stern. I wonder if Blythe will grow up to be like her mother, and then I wonder if I will grow up to be like my mother, and then I look over at Erin—who is too young to be having deep thoughts like mine but who is already wearing a headband like her mother—and I think, *Erin is the luckiest one.*

Our parents don't realize, but *White Christmas* is an educational film. It is the film where we learn to become critics, where we learn to dissect women's bodies the way we will dissect frogs and fetal pigs in high school biology class. (There is that much concentration involved, that much eye-mind coordination.) It is also the film where I will come to revise my previous hypothesis about beauty. The face still takes precedence over other parts of the body, but the face alone is not enough. We have all heard it said before, dismissively, as a consolation prize: *Well, she does have a very pretty face.* This is like the comment *She had a nice handbag* when what you really mean to say is *Did you see what a hideous dress?*

The body *is* the dress, and there are genes under it that you never see (mixed in with the blood and guts), and this is because the dress-body is sewn onto the actual body the way the dresses on some dolls are inseparable from the dolls themselves. They don't come with a change of clothes. The most you can do is accessorize: Add a necklace. Paint the nails. Maybe—if you are really daring—cut the hair.

Blythe begins: "Who would you rather be—Betty or Judy?" She freezes the frame so we can see them standing together, performing their sister act in the turquoise dresses with the enormous, feathered fans.

"Which one is Betty again?" Sometimes Erin has trouble following.

"That's Rosemary Clooney," I say, springing up to stand beside the television and using my finger like a pointer. "She's playing Betty, the older sister. Over here is Vera-Ellen." I am so enamored of her hyphenated first name I cannot say it without smiling or without wondering how it would sound if I went around as Julie-Marie. "She is playing Judy, the younger sister. Got it now?"

"Got it," Erin nods. "I pick Judy."

"Me, too," Blythe quickly concurs.

When Blythe and I watch this movie together—since Erin's visits are few—we both pick Judy, then squabble over the fact that someone will have to play Betty if we are going to act out the parts. Blythe says since I'm the older cousin, it only makes sense that I should play the older sister, but I protest each time and make us do rock-paper-scissors to decide. This time I take a different approach. "That's fine with me. I'm going to be Betty. I like Betty."

"She's bigger," Blythe observes, "but you're bigger, too, so . . ." Her demeanor changes from smug to something else. *Pity maybe?* I don't like pity one bit.

"That's just because I'm growing so fast," I say. "One day both of you will catch up."

"No, it's not *taller,*" Blythe explains. The sisters are dancing and singing now, twirling around while the two men in the audience gawk and grin. She stands beside the television and gestures to their bodies. "Betty is bigger—wider through the shoulders. Think about the fancy dance numbers, like 'The Best Things Happen When You're Dancing,' or 'Mandy.' Only Judy performs, and that's because Judy is small, light on her feet."

All at once, I feel an urgent need to defend Betty. "I think she's beautiful," I say. "I like when she sings 'Love, You Didn't Do Right by Me' in that black velvet dress with the long white gloves. You can tell Rosemary Clooney's a great singer—a lot more vocally talented than Vera-Ellen, or at least better trained." Though I try to keep emotion out of it and simply parrot things my mother has said, I know in my heart I want to be the slender woman with the high blond ponytail, weightless as a bird when Danny Kaye tosses her into the air.

Blythe and I resume our seats on either side of Erin, facing each other more than the television screen. "Rosemary Clooney had an hourglass figure," Blythe remarks, thinking I won't know the term. "It was more popular in her time than it is in ours."

"So what?" I retort.

"Well, I don't know if you know—" Blythe pauses now for effect—"but she got really fat when she got old. My mom and I saw her on a talk show."

I try not to react to this news, try not to allow it to alter my impression of her, my second-favorite actress in the film. "What happened to Vera-Ellen then?"

"Oh, I don't know. But my mother says she was on record as having the smallest waist in Hollywood."

"What record?"

She shrugs. "I guess they have one."

The words leap out of my mouth, like oil from a frying pan; I instantly regret them. "Well, I don't care what you say—Rosemary Clooney has a *very pretty face.*"

My cousin grins at me. "Oh, definitely." Her icy blue eyes gleam. "I agree."

In a little while, Aunt Sharon comes and stands behind the sofa, brushing Blythe's hair the way she often does. It is long and thick and golden like a fairy tale princess. Blythe has even played Rapunzel in her school play.

"When this is over," Sharon offers, "I can show you a video of the three of you playing together a couple of years ago. Do you remember when Daddy got his Camcorder?"

Blythe leaps to her feet, hair spreading around her like a superhero's cape. "Let's watch it now!" she pleads.

"But you're watching *White Christmas.*"

"We want to see it! We want to see it!" Erin joins in, and not wanting to seem like a spoil sport, I silently nod my head. Inside, though, my stomach tilts on a whirligig, and my heart grows loud in my ears.

"All right, then." She holds her thermos in one hand and browses the VHS shelf with the other. "I think this was the last time all the cousins were here," Sharon says, with a casualness I instinctively distrust. She slides the dark tape down the machine's bright throat. We listen for the click before a grainy image appears.

"There you are," she announces. "See? It's muddy, so you're all on the steps in your Easter dresses."

Three girls are standing in a row. They wear pastel dresses and patent leather shoes. One dons a bonnet, and another has bows in her hair. But I can't see it, or believe it, or both. "Which one is me?" I blurt out.

Now Sharon takes a sip of her coffee and points to the screen. "Don't you recognize yourself?" The tallest girl, the *biggest* girl, has brown curls fastened with pink barrettes. Her glasses are pink and smudged and sit catawampus on her nose. One of her front teeth is missing, and the other is just pushing through, and her hands fidget with the low pink sash set off to the side of the dress meant to resemble a sunrise.

This is the (fifth) great sadness of my life, and I have no words to express it.

"You look like Little Orphan Annie!" Erin squeals.

"But *she* had red hair," Blythe corrects, "and could dance."

Memo: I have discovered what all beautiful women have in common. They know how to move their bodies in time with music, and even if there were no music at all, they would know how to move their bodies. They are the music. Vera-Ellen is more beautiful than Rosemary Clooney. I don't want it to be true, but it is. She has a more musical body, less solid and more liquid, so she flows across space instead of clunking through it. I also have a corollary hypothesis that beautiful women are more likely to die young. (This is not a consolation, just a fact.) Vera-Ellen, for instance, is already dead, but Rosemary Clooney is alive and well. I looked them up at the library after school. I think the more beautiful you are, the more tragic your death will be. You have to go out like a shooting star.

⧗

It is my last year of lessons at the Fiorini Ski School. My cousin Blythe is in my division now, and unfortunately, she is a prodigy on skis. (*See how she trumps me in everything!*) I am more cautious by comparison, less sure on my feet, meandering down the mountain in my slow zig-zag, while Blythe whizzes past, her body a straight razor slicing through the trees.

"Blythe is a good skier," I tell my Aunt Sharon when we are stuck on the chair lift together.

"I know," she replies without turning her head.

"I like the way her hair flies out behind her like a magic carpet when she speeds down the mountain. She has really pretty hair."

I am saying what I think grown-ups want to hear, complimenting them on something impressive that they feel responsible for. After all, my mother always said, teary-eyed as she tucked me into bed: *You are my greatest accomplishment.*

"Did you have hair like that when you were a kid?" I ask Aunt Sharon.

"I did. I had beautiful golden hair that everyone said looked like sunshine." Her voice never lilts, and it never wavers. She keeps her eyes trained straight ahead.

"And my mother—did she have—"

"*No,*" Sharon intercedes, a little too quick, a little too certain. "She did not."

"So, she had dark hair then? I can never seem to find any pictures."

"Yes. Dark hair. Dark skin. She wasn't fair the way Steve and I were, and she didn't like to have her picture taken." A new intensity creeps into her words, the faintest suggestion that Aunt Sharon is actually enjoying our conversation.

"But what was she like—my mother—*overall?*"

"She was . . ." Sharon takes a long pause, exactly the way her daughter would. She slips off her gloves and bends a piece of gum slowly, dramatically, into her mouth. "I would say she was something of a *Plain Jane.*"

The words strike like a match and burn all the way down to the pit of my stomach. The *fire pit*—where the ugliest feelings are stored.

Later, in Sharon and Thor's motor home, we gather at the small table and eat goulash.

"Guess what?" Blythe grins. "I'm starting ice skating lessons."

"Oh," I say. "Why?"

"My friend Sabrina's sister Celeste is an ice skater, and she's so good she's skating in France right now. If I'm good enough, I could go to France, too."

"We'll see," Thor says in his father-voice that means *Probably not.*

"Julie's starting at a new dance studio in the fall. She'll be combining ballet, tap, and jazz with a bit of gymnastics and aerobics." My mother presses down so hard that her plastic fork snaps. Sharon hands her another from the box.

"Have you ever done gymnastics before?" Blythe asks.

"No. But it's only a small part of the class."

"Can you do this?" Blythe moves into the narrow aisle behind the driver's seat and bends backwards, effortlessly, into a bridge. "It's fun! See? Are you watching? You can even walk around like this," and she raises her feet and hands.

When Blythe sits down again, her face is pink as a dog's tongue from where all the blood has rushed to her head. No one says anything, but Sharon leans over and kisses her daughter's cheek. It is my (sixth) great sadness in life that I don't know how to leave a room yet. I always wait for someone to excuse me, someone to tell me I'm done. But I want to stand up right now, more than anything—without apology and without regret—open the door and let the cold air in, not even bother to close it as I step out into the moonlit snow.

Memo: Marilyn Monroe died of an overdose, a real-life Sleeping Beauty no one could wake up. Grace Kelly lost control of her car and crashed. She was called Her Serene Highness the Princess of Monaco in all the papers. I hope she at least died on a moonlit mountain road with a beautiful view of the sea. My father thinks it's unhealthy to spend so much time researching these deaths, and my mother thinks it's unbecoming to be morbid. ("Unbecoming" is another way of saying "unbeautiful," but nicer, I suppose.) What I think—what I've come to believe based on loads of research—is that I'm going to live a very long time. It's possible that I may live forever.

ENCORE

Dangerous is the epiphany that you are old enough to have a history. This is a danger like no other, except perhaps the danger of that primeval epiphany: You have a body. *Have? Are?* No one is sure, not even Descartes, but he will serve as whipping boy for all our accusations of embodiment. Bodies discombobulated like buoys on the waves. Betty bodies. Judy bodies. Bodies scrutinized by wide-eyed movie-goers. Bodies bending like willow trees. Motile bodies. Sessile bodies. Bodies with waists that set Hollywood records. Bodies that shimmy while their voices trill. Voices that trill while their bodies shimmy. (Jitterbug bodies are among the most compelling bodies.) Aimless bodies. Automaton bodies. Bodies cleaving to other bodies. Bodies practicing Solitaire. Somehow, we suspect, Descartes had a hand in it—hand or mind. *Do I think therefore I am, or am I therefore I think?* This is not unlike the Prince's question to Cinderella at the Ball: *Do I love you because you're beautiful, or are you beautiful because I love you?* The idea of a beautiful body. The idea of a not-so-beautiful body. Other ideas apart from the body but in which the body is implicated, charged: Mercury in retrograde. Retrograde amnesia. A gavel's strike. A grim prognosis. Light as a feather, stiff as a board. A face dissolving in a photograph—when faces were still captured on film. A starlet, a convertible, a mountain road: nothing but a fleck in the darkness. The stellar body is an interstellar body indeed. Starlight: sweet heavenly body.

PART II

"The truth is in the teeth," the dentist claims. He is tall and tapered like a candle; he wears a green mask over his mouth. "They are the longest-lasting feature of our species. They carry the body's secrets."

"I thought that was the tongue," I say.

Now he lets out a hearty laugh. The mask crinkles around his lips. I commit to memory the contents of his window ledge: aloe plant, abalone shell, driftwood.

"You're an intriguing little girl." He states it like a fact, not a compliment. He seems like a prophet to me, a man who should be standing on a mountaintop.

"Thank you," I say. My mother has taught me nothing if not good manners.

As he cleans my teeth, Dr. Watts describes the mouth like a magic kingdom. He is in love with his profession, the way some men love their wives and children, the way prophets love the Word of God. "Did you know that paleontologists use teeth to identify fossils? From teeth, they can tell what the creature was, what it ate, who its family members were."

He holds the little mirror on the silver stem inside my mouth. In the next room, I hear my mother chatting with the receptionist. I practice my best concentration, the dial in my mind turning her loud voice down.

"I hear you're the finest speller in first grade," he says. "Can you spell *teeth*?" I nod. "*Gums*?" I nod again. "What about *enamel?*" I think on it, then nod again. "Well, that's very good." Dr. Watts wipes his utensils and offers me a sip of water. "Do you think you could spell *deciduous?*"

I have never heard this word before. It comes over me like a wave, successive splashes of yellow and green. "What does it mean?" I ask.

"Something temporary—like leaves on a tree, like your first set of teeth." I have lost one tooth already, and another is loose. "These are your *deciduous* teeth," he tells me, "but your permanent teeth are on their way."

My tongue moves to the new space at the front of my mouth where the air rushes in when I try to whistle. "Do you know the Tooth Fairy?" I ask him. It is almost time for my mother, with her dark pink lips and full set of permanent teeth, to take my place in this chair.

"You mean personally?"

I nod.

"Well, I think I've bumped into him at a conference or two. Someone may have introduced us."

"The Tooth Fairy is a man?" This possibility has not occurred to me before. I thought *fairy* was a girl-word, like *princess* or *ballerina.*

Dr. Watts, guilty for revealing a secret that only the teeth should know, looks away and pretends to be interested in my X-rays. "Well, it was a long time ago," he says. "I could have been mistaken."

"It's OK," I reassure him. "I won't tell anyone." But I like the idea that I am privy to this truth, like the truth of angels, who are always glowing women on the Christmas tree but seem to be only glowing men in the Bible.

"We're all done here," he smiles, his mask removed. "You have strong, happy teeth, young lady. Let's make sure they stay that way."

You are seven years old and coming into your calling. For you, the truth is in the words you study in the dic-

tionary, under pretense of learning their forms. Yes, it delights you—the surprise of the "p" in "receipt," the double "l" at the conclusion of "quill." You are interested in their relationships—how the quill might be used to write the receipt in a careful cursive you haven't learned yet. But there is also the texture of the words, their glint in the light, their cadence as they fall upon the ear. While your mother quizzes you at the kitchen table, you consider the bodies of words, their relative beauties. You consider their heft and height and the other words contained within them—"heat" inside "sheath," "evil" inside "devil." Words, you marvel, are like nesting dolls, able to stand apart and also fit together.

⧗

For Thanksgiving we travel. We become like pilgrims (*p-i-l-g-r-i-m-s*), with my father at the helm and my grandmother beside him. *She like the quill, he like the receipt she has written . . .* My mother and I squeeze our knees close in the upholstered back seat of the company car. Together we spell and sing and stare off into the distance.

Aunt Linda is our destination. Soon, we will see her where she lives alone in a one-bedroom apartment—not a wife yet, and not a homeowner either. *Do you have to be married to have a house?* But I have been chided for asking about marriage before, as in the last year—when I was six and still simple-minded—and I studied the ring on her right middle finger: "Is that your wedding ring? Why do you wear it there, on the wrong hand?"

"Aunt Linda may be sensitive about that fact," my father said. "It is better to ask people about what they have than about what they are lacking."

Aunt Linda has my mother's name. Both their mothers christened them *Linda,* and since my mother married my father and since my aunt is still a tenant and not a wife, they both sign their checks *Linda Wade,* though the script is different just as the letter that comes between: *Linda M.* my mother, *Linda A.* my aunt.

If my father calls out in a room, both women will turn and answer. This fact surprises me also—that there aren't enough names for everyone to have her own.

Aunt Linda wears an apron dusted with flour. Beneath it, a mauve (*m-a-u-v-e*) sweater and winter white slacks. She hugs us each like we might break, and then we scatter—which is close to *shatter* but not quite. *Scatter* is a movement word; *shatter* refers to glass.

"Mama, I've got a nice hot cup of coffee for you," Aunt Linda says, leading my grandmother to an oversized chair. My father hangs up his hat and sets to work sliding the leaf into the dining room table. In the kitchen, my mother dons an apron, adjusts the station on the radio. When I perch on the stool at the pass-through window, two Lindas mash potatoes side by side, two Lindas arrange *hors d'oeuvres* (*spelling unknown*) without speaking.

"Aunt Linda, I was wondering—"

"On my bookshelf," she smiles, pleased with her psychic powers.

I bolt down the hallway and into her room. There are bells on the doorknob that jingle as I enter; these are not just for Christmas but for all year round. Breathless, I spin until my eyes fix on the brightly colored nesting doll (also called a *Russian doll* and another word that starts with "m" that I can't pronounce yet). My joy is like gratitude, my heart like the horn of plenty. I kneel on the carpet and begin to un-nest them. This is how it is to be human: to have more than one person inside you. First, I thought it was the years of life, like the little one-year-old inside the slightly bigger two-year-old, the simple-minded six-year-old inside the complex-minded seven-year-old. But now I know otherwise. As I pair each doll-body with its doll-head, I think about the me that is bad at dancing and the me that is good at spelling and the me the teacher thinks is quiet, even though I am full to brimming with words she has never asked me to say. I think also about the me my father loves to take to the park, the me my grandmother says reminds her of her dead husband, the me my mother so often finds disappointing. I was not born with natural curly hair. I have dimples, true, but two left feet. Despite the best lessons and home permanents, I will never be a Shirley Temple.

I lay the dolls out and line them up on the bed. I like to admire them just as they are—nameless, with faces that never change. The same cannot be said for the rest of us. On the nightstand, a younger version of my grandmother stands beside a younger version of my Aunt Linda. It is the mother-daughter tea at Linda's sorority (*s-o-r-o-r-i-t-y*), a place where girls go to become beautiful in college. Aunt Linda has pale gold hair that slants across her cheeks and pale thin arms she never shows now, even in the heat of summer. Grandma June has dark hair spun high like a layer cake and wears a soft pink corsage pinned to the breast of her suit. I wouldn't know it was them if I hadn't been told. When my father summons me to the table, I am still sitting here on my knees.

I turn to him, hesitant at the doorframe, and all I can think to say is, "Why does Aunt Linda sleep in a little girl's bed?" There is the wicker headboard, the flowered quilt, the narrow width for only one body. It is like my bed, or the bed borrowed by Goldilocks. I glance again at her pale gold hair. My father shakes his head but doesn't answer.

Your mouth is always full of words, but sometimes they are hidden, your teeth like trees in a forest of unsayable things. There are many ways to imagine it. The teeth are trees, or they are wood pilings in the water, your mouth the harbor where words come to rest and wait. The words are boats, like the kind you watch from your kitchen window. There are sailboats, which are light and breezy with bright-colored sails (the colors of Matryoshka dolls). There are freighters, too, big ships that are pulled along by small ships—the way your father is pulled along by your mother. These ships are called tugs, named for what they do. You have never seen a cruise ship, but your Aunt Linda has traveled on a floating hotel all the way to Alaska and back again. Your Great Aunt Ruth comes from Canada by ship, a large ferry with a special name—the Victoria Clipper. Other words come to mind, other words you are storing in your harbor-mouth: skiff, yacht, catamaran. The last one gleams red and gold.

⧗

My first friend is Joy, and when I say her name, I swell with the feeling the word conveys. I wonder if her mother finds it hard to scold her, struggles with an exclamation like *Joy, you disgust me! Clean this up this instant!* Joy's mother's name is Melody, so I can only imagine she sings both punishment and praise. She has wild black curls and slippers stitched with beaded dragons. Her long, taut (*t-a-u-t*) body moves through the house like a dancer, which is the way Joy moves. They are women who have swallowed grace like a tablet, and now, having dissolved, the grace moves through them, a river flowing under their skin.

This will be my first time traveling away from home without my parents. My mother makes carrot cake and cries over the pan. My father warns me again about the Strangers, who are everywhere lurking with malice (which contains the name *Alice*) in their hearts. When I have packed my small, blue-and-white vinyl suitcase, I set it at the foot of my bed. This is like the military. My mother comes for inspection.

"Where is your deodorant?" she says.

"You said it was a secret, so I didn't bring it. I didn't want anyone to see."

"So, what will you do when you're sweating in the sun? When you're playing hard, and the odor starts to fill your clothes?"

I stand still, petrified like fossil.

"Do you *want* to smell bad?" She bends over me and stares into my eyes.

"No—but no one else in second grade wears deodorant."

"Well, you're different," my mother decrees. "Sometimes for the best, and sometimes for the worst, but I can't have a smelly daughter. Now," smoothing my hair, "go get your Speed Stick from the bathroom, and we'll hide it in the zippered pocket."

Joy's father steers the boat away from the dock while my parents stand in the harbor, waving. "When I grow up, I want to live on a houseboat," Joy says. "Can you imagine waking up every day on the sea?"

I can't imagine exactly, but I have always wanted a waterbed. Now I see that Joy's dream is better: the boat like a cradle, the waves rocking the sleepers to and fro, a lullaby (*l-u-l-l-a-b-y*) of sea gulls and passing storms.

"Let's fall asleep," she exclaims, "and when we wake up, we can pretend it's a brand-new day on our very own houseboat!"

Downstairs in a room like a giant sofa—nothing but cushions from wall to wall and little round windows for peering through—we stretch out and close our eyes. "Do you really want to sleep, or only make-believe sleep?" I ask.

"Whichever," she says. I admire the way Joy is casual about everything.

Then, her little brother Raphael climbs up on the couch in the room made of couch, and we all huddle together like shipwreck survivors. This is another game we play. Soon, we fall asleep because the sea beneath us is rhythmic like a poem; later, Melody tickles our feet to tell us, *We're here! We've arrived!* Soon, there will be a fire on the island, fresh salmon and salty fries, a sky full of stars, and a night full of stories.

"Use the bathroom if you need to," she says. "We won't come back to the boat until late."

⧗

I think of my deodorant now, how my mother says I should *take every opportunity to freshen up.* "I'll meet you upstairs," I whisper to Joy, twitchy with the first truth I cannot tell her.

"OK," she says, suspecting nothing, guiding Raphael, chubby and unsteady in his bright orange vest, along the narrow stairs toward the light.

Even my palms are sweating as I slip the hard plastic capsule into my hand, conceal myself behind the sliding door. As I unbutton my shirt, I notice the goose bumps on my arms, a prickling sensation that has nothing to do with cold. It is the feeling of wanting neither thing at once. A renunciation (*r-e-n-u-n-c-i-a-t-i-o-n*) of some kind. Fearful to disregard my mother's instructions and yet, fearful to remain here, in this dark, cramped place, rubbing this grown-up paste on my body. My father talks about *the devil and the deep blue sea.* He says sometimes we are caught between them. I think I know now what he means.

Just then, as I am standing in my white undershirt with the small blue violets, one hand straight up like I'm hailing a cab in a movie, the other pressing the blocked powder into the hollow place under my arm, Melody opens the door. "Oh, excuse me!" she exclaims, like a reflex, like I am older than I am, deserving of my privacy. Now she pauses. Now her eyes widen, big and brown and full of concern. "Julie," she says, "what on earth are you doing?"

"Nothing," I say, which is a word that never dissolves easily on my tongue. It is a terrible aspirin of a word, a word with consequences.

"Is that deodorant?"

"My mother says it's OK. My mother says I can have it."

"But you're eight years old! No eight-year-old needs deodorant. Besides," she says, softening, "it's nothing but chemicals. There are other ways to stay clean and dry. *Natural* ways." Melody's long, slender fingers extend toward me. I understand this is a gentle confiscation (*c-o-n-f-i-s-c-a-t-i-o-n*).

"Will I get it back at the end of the trip?" I ask, beginning to shiver. This, too, has nothing to do with cold.

She doesn't answer. Then, over her shoulder, like an afterthought: "All things in good time, my dear."

Most secrets you have to carry with you, hard as the teeth in your mouth. You grow a list of things you cannot tell your mother. It is not the same list of things you cannot tell your father, though there are points of overlap. For instance, you cannot tell your mother how you have invented an alternate family. As a woman who struggled to have a child—a woman who could have only one—your mother would take it personally, this need for other children in the house, other parents. But with your father, hunting for sand crabs on a Saturday afternoon, you can talk about your sisters and brothers. You can tell him how Matthew is in the military (the way your father was during Vietnam), how Kristen has red hair she wears in a flip (like Laura Petrie), how Vanessa is a dancer and just got fitted for braces. There is one sister, though—your twin sister—who you must never say a word about. She knows all your secrets, even the most shameful ones. In a few years, she will also need braces.

⧗

I sit with Kellie in the best tree in our grandmother's backyard. We like to pretend we are Mary Lennox and Dickon looking over the wall into the secret garden. Sometimes we climb down and pick rhubarb (*r-h-u-b-a-r-b*), which grows red and wild in the untended flowerbeds. We rinse it with the hose, being older now and a little afraid of the dirt. Then, we move higher into the rockery, just out of view, where the next neighbor's gate is wrapped with a chain, cinched with a padlock. This is where we like to pause, tugging the rhubarb between our teeth—sometimes sweet, but mostly sour—and play our private game.

I have hidden my best treasure here, wedged between the rocks. It is something I found in an old box belonging to our mother. The keychain is a huge red plastic heart, with the word LOVE printed in tall white letters. Attached are no fewer than fifty keys. Most of them are ordinary to look at, gold or gray with tiny teeth made to fit some furtive lock. But one is blue as a peacock feather, smaller than all the others and many times more beguiling (*b-e-g-u-i-l-i-n-g*). I have already tried it in every lock I can think of, including the padlock that beckons over my shoulder. *There wouldn't be a key without a lock, would there?* They must make the lock first, and then the way to get inside.

"You're a good sleuth," Kellie tells me. "Someday you'll find the door for every key."

"It's more than doors, though. There are boxes with locks, even diaries."

"Sure," she agrees. "But things tend to look like what they are. You can tell a car key from a house key after all. And diaries have the smallest keys, so if you were being interrogated, say, you could swallow that key and never have to open the book where your biggest secrets are stored."

Kellie has a point there. Many sleuths before me have had to make bold moves in sticky situations. They have had to hold their tongues when it mattered most, to practice silence like a dance, or a tricky piano piece—silence like a concerto (*c-o-n-c-e-r-t-o*) by Grieg.

"Can you imagine if I died," I say, "and the doctor took an X-ray, and there in my belly, the size of a bone, he found one of those long, elegant, skeleton keys?"

Kellie smiles at me. She can picture it, too. Unlike most people we know, she appreciates the way death and beauty sometimes go together. This is no one's fault. It's just something that happens that no one likes to say.

"My turn," Kellie whispers, dislodging the hourglass she has pilfered from Trivial Pursuit. "Same rules as always: you have till the sand runs out to reveal a secret or announce a new mystery."

Isn't a secret sometimes a mystery? And isn't a mystery almost always a secret?

"Well," I say softly, wondering how the words will sound when I speak them aloud. "This is a secret, I guess. I've never told anyone else."

Kellie leans forward, looking like the gymnastic (*g-y-m-n-a-s-t-i-c*) orphan with the long side braids in the movie we love called *Annie*.

"You know our sister Kristen, the one with the red hair?"

"I know her. Of course I know her." Without using words, Kellie conveys a phrase our father often murmurs, something about two different people *being cut from the same cloth*.

"Well, I think I love her."

"You should. She's your sister."

"No. I think about her more than the others. I think about her the way you think about Todd Lucas at school."

Kellie adores this blond-haired boy, his baseball cap and tight blue jeans, the way his last name is also a first name.

Now, for the first time since I've known (created) her, my sister is silent. She wears an expression like she has just swallowed a key, the bad taste of metal in her mouth. "At night," I tell her, "when you're sleeping, I sometimes wander over to Kristen's room. She's usually just sitting at the vanity, brushing her hair. I think she's perfect—like a model but way more interesting. I can't help it. She's like Christmas: that red hair and those bright green eyes."

"This doesn't make any sense," Kellie says, blinking hard.

"I know. It doesn't." *So maybe my secret is partly a mystery, too.*

Your diary doesn't have a lock. One day far in the future, your mother will discover it, and she will instruct you to make it disappear. She will find herself "scandalized" by the content. She will tell you that everything you have written "casts the whole family in a negative light." But long before this happens, you will become adept at tearing certain pages out. It is enough to write the words themselves, bold in your new cursive, to press your pencil tip into the white spaces between the neat blue lines, to see what you are most longing to say. There are many pages devoted to Ann Reinking, the dancer who played Grace Farrell in Annie. *You love the part where Daddy Warbucks, who loves her the way you do and is not her father, tells her that her teeth are crooked. She offers to have them fixed, but he tells her he likes them crooked. This is a sad truth for you to face—the fact that your own teeth are as straight as the pickets on fences, that the dentist tells you time after time that you will never need braces. In your mind, it is the same as saying you will never be loved.*

⧗

In the summer, my mother sends me to day camp. With Joy away in California, riding horses at her grandparents' ranch, camp is a concerted effort to find new friends, a preemptive strike against the failure to fit in. This is why, I reason, *camp* must be short for *campaign*. My mother has launched this campaign (*c-a-m-p-a-i-g-n*) in favor of a more appropriate daughter.

"I'm not lonely," I insist, even though it is only a partial truth and sits unevenly on the bridge of my tongue.

"I don't care if you're lonely or not." Perhaps this is a partial truth, too. "I care that you stop talking to yourself and start living here with the rest of us—here in the real world."

I raise my eyebrows, and Kellie recedes to the background.

At Camp Long, all the counselors have self-chosen names, names like Squirrel and Inch. No matter how many times I ask them, they won't reveal their real names, the names their parents gave them. This, I'm told, is their prerogative (*p-r-e-r-o-g-a-t-i-v-e*). They are grown-ups and entitled to their secrets. I look down and frown at the small square of adhesive pressed to my chest, the way I have no say at all in the words someone else has printed with a Sharpie: *Julie Wade*. I had no say at all when my parents chose them.

"But if the counselors get to name themselves," I protest—"just for camp, just for the duration . . ." Inch is shorter than I am, even though she is old, a grouchy leprechaun of a woman who scrunches her face at words longer than two syllables. "Doesn't it only seem fair that we should get to name ourselves, too?"

In military fashion, she takes my second name first, inverts the two to make a point about power: "*Wade,*" she commands, "go stand at the back of the line."

Then, there is Spider, after whom I will never complain again about camp. Even the word *after* goes slack as fishing line when I say it. Spider must stay always in present tense. I cannot imagine my life beyond her, a future that does not include her face.

The strange thing is that Kellie has warned me about this. She shakes her head as I lie to our mother about the special tasks I've been given, the imaginary mandate that I must arrive early each morning at Camp Long. Kellie pinches me as I perch on the hillside, watching the counselors gather together with clipboards in hand, coffee steaming in Styrofoam cups. I scan the landscape for Spider and spot her at once, her dark red hair—far more auburn than Anne Shirley's carrot top or Nancy Drew's elusive, titian color. True red, like the flame in the lantern at church, the one that burns for all time and must never be extinguished (*e-x-t-i-n-g-u-i-s-h-e-d*).

"It's like a signature," I whisper to Kellie. "The thing that makes her distinctive. A sign she'll never be lost in a crowd."

"She's not even *your* counselor," Kellie sighs. "If you're not careful, you're going to find yourself in a world of trouble." She digs her fingernail into the gash on my knee, a quick way to ensure I'm listening.

"Since when do you sound exactly like Mom?"

"Think about it, Julie. This is worse than the thing with Kristen. Spider is a real person." She looks at me, bright eyes and tight braids with ribbons woven through. "You aren't just allowed to love whoever you want."

"Why not? Why aren't you?" But Kellie begins to vaporize, the way she does, so I bite my lip and look for four-leaf clovers.

"You're here early," a soft voice says. I raise my eyes, and there is Spider, peering down at me from beneath her shiny visor.

"Oh." The word lingers on my lips until I lick it away. "I'm sorry." It is the only thing I can think to say. (And I *am* sorry, the way sorry is an umbrella that covers all our conflicting intentions.)

"No, it's fine," she smiles, and her teeth are big and straight and white like mine—a full mouth of them, perfect and permanent.

Unlike the other counselors, Spider brings her own cup, hand-painted it seems with stars and butterflies. "I don't like to be wasteful," she says, following my eyes. "Styrofoam is so bad for the environment."

"For the fish," I nod. "We talked about it in school, and last year we even went around spray-painting near the sewer grates with stencils that said NO DUMPING." Suddenly, it is hard to stop talking. The latch in my throat swings open, and I am thinking how this is my only chance to make my best impression. "We're very big on recycling, too, and on making sure dolphins don't get caught in the fishermen's nets."

Spider is smiling again, wider this time. I sneak a peek at her threadbare jeans, stone-washed and intentionally ragged. (This is the style, though my mother finds it appalling, refuses to let me take part.) With red magic marker, she has printed, then meticulously darkened, the word BELIEVE down the length of her thigh.

"What do you believe in?" I ask, pointing.

"Oh, lots of things. Nature. Love. Karma."

"What's that word?" I ask. It's one I don't recognize, one I'm not sure how to spell.

"Karma? Well, it's like when you do good things, and then good things happen to you. The energy we put out into the world is the energy that comes back to us."

"Is it spelled with a 'c' or a 'k'?"

"A 'k,'" she says, bemused but still smiling.

"So, with karma (*k-a-r-m-a?*)—when you do bad things—is that what they mean when they say it will come back to haunt you?"

"Kind of. Yeah." She sips her coffee and looks out over the lawn where a light morning fog rolls through. "There's this poet," Spider tells me. "I studied her in college. And she was so smart, so sensitive to everything that was happening in the world, even though she didn't go out in the world too much. Anyway, she said, *You don't have to be a house to be haunted.*"

I think this is the most profound statement I have ever heard and can't wait to record it in my diary, that precious little book without a lock or key. It wasn't even a secret so much as a revelation.

"What was her name?" I ask. "The poet?"

"Emily Dickinson," Spider says. "Isn't that a great name?"

I nod. "What's *your* name?" I want her to say it, the real name she was given, not the pretend name she has chosen. I want it to slip through, the way water snakes between the river's teeth, honest and insistent.

"Oh, it's Spider," she smiles—as if I didn't know, as if I hadn't studied everything about her, listened when the other campers called for her across the field. A pink blush mottles (*m-o-t-t-l-e-s*) her pale white cheeks. "I should have said that to begin with."

You learn that some keys are invisible. They are transferred in language, or image, and their purpose is to unlock a truth in your mind. This is like karma—karma is a key. It is easier to believe than God, who is becoming foggy, a lost form in a deep valley. While you cannot pray to karma exactly, you understand it as a quiet law. Because of Spider, you spend a lot of time at the library reading about Emily Dickinson. You are perplexed because there seems to be only one picture of her. You wish you had a picture of Spider. But if you could choose—would you rather have a picture, which would last forever, or her real name, which would last forever in a different way but ensure you could find her in the phonebook? Spider's lush red hair is proof, to your mind, of her excellent karma, though you wonder about her limp, the way one leg drags slightly after the other. Is this the result of something she did wrong, some Styrofoam she used before she knew any better? You wonder other things, too, things your sister insists you should not wonder. Does she have a boyfriend? What do they do together in the dark? What would it feel like to slide your hand across the skin that appears beneath the frays in her denim, like light through slats in the floor?

⧗

The next year a new girl returns to camp in the guise of my body. She is taller than everyone now, as tall as her own mother, who commends her height and has been known to exclaim, "We're hoping for Nicole Kidman here, or Gwyneth Paltrow!" These are not names she recognizes, though she suspects they are movie stars. Whoever they are, she trusts they are tall and blond.

Though I am longing to see Spider, I have already loved someone in the interim (*i-n-t-e-r-i-m*), someone I was not supposed to love—my fourth-grade teacher. I have also failed to love someone I was expected to love—my first boyfriend. I wear Lee's friendship bracelet around my wrist, practice thinking of him when I fall asleep at night. But soon my mind drifts back to Mrs. Miller, ascending the staircase in her spacious house—which always resembles Barbie's dream house, no matter how hard I try to make it otherwise. She is clad in a lavender nightgown that trails behind her, with slippers and a robe to match.

When she opens the door to her bedroom, Mr. Miller is there, propped on the soft white pillows, reading the newspaper in his undershirt, his neckline rimmed with coarse black hairs. I squint to squeeze him out of the picture, but he always returns, resilient as a toothache or a canker sore. He flashes her an eager smile, then reaches over to switch off the light.

Now during free time, I linger on the hill, hoping for a chance to talk to Spider. As a cover, I have my notebook with me, and even an alibi (*a-l-i-b-i*): I'm pretending to write a field guide for future visitors to Camp Long.

"Hello!" she waves. "Can you remind me of your name again?"

"It's Julie," I say, my eyes averted, but my heart climbing up in my throat.

"That's right. What are you working on?" Spider inquires. She tucks her one sore leg under the other and perches beside me on the grass. I glance at her quickly, like small sips of water. The worst thing is to be caught gulping. I notice that she is wearing a white t-shirt with a v-shaped neck. I notice that a silver charm dangles against her smooth, exposed skin. I notice that her nails are coated with gloss.

"Oh, just a project," I offer, trying to sound nonchalant (*n-o-n-c-h-a-l-a-n-t*). "I want to write a detailed guide to the campsite, maybe have it distributed to future visitors." For some reason, when I'm nervous, I lean on my biggest words. They're like crutches, which my father says make your armpits sore if you rely on them too long.

"What a nice idea!" she says. "Will you draw maps, too?"

"Maybe, but I'm more of a wordsmith than a visual artist."

Spider sits beside me for a little while, scanning the landscape for campers gone wild or astray. "Did you make that bracelet yourself?" she asks, and all at once a door—a portal to a new kind of conversation—begins to materialize.

"Actually, my boyfriend made it for me," I reply.

Now Spider regards me in a different light. I can hear the shift in her voice, the note of reverence. "Really? You have a boyfriend? That's wonderful."

"It was bound to happen," I say, "now that I'm almost eleven."

"What's he like?"

"Oh, you know—like a boyfriend." This is a harder question than it sounds, since Lee is mostly just an outline to me, a blurry apparition like the Gnostic Jesus. In some essential but inexpressible way, I didn't believe Lee's body was made of the same earthly substance as mine.

"Do *you* have a boyfriend?" I ask, and this is easier now because I have established myself as an experienced woman, a potential confidant (*c-o-n-f-i-d-a-n-t*).

"I did," she sighs, "but we broke up. I probably shouldn't be wearing this necklace now, but I like it so much I kept it anyway."

Spider has granted me license to look, to peer at the piece of silver glinting against her collarbones. It is, of all things, a key.

"Does it open something?" I whisper, the world becoming too loud a place again, threatening to drown out our conversation.

"No. It's just—symbolic." Her eyes are green and dreamy, but now they are moist, too, like she might cry. "You know, I think he was saying he had the key to my heart."

"Then, why did he give it to you? Shouldn't he have kept it?"

Spider looks at me, her eyes growing wide with surprise. "I never—" she furrows her brow—"I guess I never thought of it that way."

"Do you want to know a secret?" I say. It is more of a lie than a secret, but sometimes the lines between these are blurry, too, the truth itself an apparition.

Spider nods.

"My real name isn't Julie."

"It isn't?"

"No. My real name is *Juliet,* like the girl Romeo loved. It's old-fashioned, so I don't use it. I've actually never told anyone before."

Where Spider touches my arm, the little white hairs rise up, ecstatic. "I promise," she whispers, "that I won't tell anyone."

"Thank you," I say. "May I ask about your real name?" My mother has taught me nothing if not good manners.

Spider looks over her shoulder, then out at the field, then back again, her dreamy green eyes coming to rest on mine. "All right," she concedes. "But you can't tell anyone, or it'll take all the fun out of the camp names."

I smile into her face like a flower drenched in sunlight. "I promise," I say.

"It's Andrea."

"I've never heard that name before," I murmur, forgetting to let the air pass through to my lungs.

"Spelled like *ANN-dree-uh,*" she says, "but pronounced differently: *On-DRAY-uh.*"

It is the most extraordinary name I will ever learn, better than any princess or protagonist (*p-r-o-t-a-g-o-n-i-s-t*). "Mum's the word," she tells me, a long finger with a tapered nail pressed gently across her lips.

Spider raises herself to standing and pulls a whistle out of her pocket. I marvel that her name is as red as her hair, not like a candy apple or a cartoon balloon, but deeper, darker—something sacred even—blood on an altar or a sword.

"All right, everybody! Gather around!"

Andrea is the only word I write in my notebook. *A-N-D-R-E-A.* It becomes my first mantra, the key to an unseen door.

In school, you learn there is a text and a subtext. The teacher says there is always a subject and a theme. The theme runs under the subject like a dark river. You picture it like the Red Sea. Your job as the reader is to part the subject with your staff, to split the waters between what is obvious and what is only implied. In your first essay of fifth grade, you will explain what you learned at Camp Long. For instance: Water lilies are not free-floating, as you once believed, but tethered to the base of the pond. This is a subject. The themes beneath it, the themes that only the best and most intrepid readers will recognize, are as follows: Beauty is never unconditional; nothing is as it appears; the surface and the sub-terrain often contradict each other; desire has deep roots that are not easily severed.

In middle school, the Girl with your name becomes obvious. For years, she was only an implication, but now, in the combination class, eighth-graders seek her out—a patsy, a stick in the mud, a testing ground for a series of appalling (*a-p-p-a-l-l-i-n-g*) experiments. She will have her hair singed with an antique Zippo. She will have her arms profanely graffitied with Magic Marker. She will learn to wear a box over her head at lunchtime while someone else devours her tuna and pickles. Even the seventh-graders find her at times an easy target.

"What does a doorbell say?" Nancy asks, bounding toward her through the parking lot.

"Is this a riddle, or do you really want to know—"

Before she can finish her sentence, the classmate stabs her hard in each breast with the point of her finger. "*Ding! Dong!*"

"Why did you do that?" the Girl asks, her nipples throbbing.

"I don't know," Nancy murmurs, hanging her head. "Peer pressure, I guess."

"You don't have to succumb to it," the Girl promises.

"Are you fucking kidding me?" Nancy looks up again, disbelieving, and punches each breast hard with her fist. "*Ding! Dong!*"

The Girl will learn to spend a good deal of time standing outside her body.

⧗

Fortunately, I have a friend named April. She is sweet and soft-spoken, some might say *juvenile,* while others might call her a *wallflower,* given that she is slow to blossom and quick to withdraw from a crowd. April goes to a different school, but sometimes we walk home together. She has long, straight hair and long, painted nails and a great fondness for makeup and tiaras. She also has a sister named Kelly, though her sister is indisputably (*i-n-d-i-s-p-u-t-a-b-l-y*) real and spells her name with a "y."

"Do you shave your legs yet?" I ask her.

"I just started," April replies, sipping from a juice box while we stand at the intersection.

I have learned to look up to April, even though many people mistake me for her older sister. She was the one I called when the bleeding began, the one who knew what I meant when I whispered, "What's the worst thing that could ever happen to a girl?" April was good that way. She was patient and kind and kept a whole drawer full of Maxi pads and panty liners she had stolen from the real Kelly. April even owned three tampons, but like me, she was afraid to use them.

"So how do you do it?" I prod. "People are starting to talk."

"Is it bad?" Her chin quivers sympathetically as she glances in my direction.

"Not terrible yet, but they've noticed the hair now, so I expect the problems will escalate."

"Well, can you borrow your mother's supplies? She must have a razor and some shaving gel."

"She doesn't," I say. "My mother doesn't shave her legs. She doesn't believe in it."

The pink bow of April's mouth unties itself into a gasp. "Julie, is your mother a hippie?"

"No, she's a Republican."

"How can she—" April fumbles for her house key, which is hidden under a crate on the front porch, the same crate where a milkman still delivers cartons (not bottles) of 1% and Sweet Acidophilus (*A-c-i-d-o-p-h-i-l-u-s*). "Are you sure?"

"I'm sure. She thinks women shaving their legs is just a scam to get us to spend more money on products we don't need. But that's easy for her to say; she doesn't grow any hair on her legs. They're as white and waxy as a pair of candles."

I can tell April is flummoxed (*f-l-u-m-m-o-x-e-d*) by this news and will probably spend some time nursing a chocolate milk as she mulls it over. "No hair at all? Not even the downy blond kind?"

"No," I say, shaking my head.

"Julie, are you sure your mother isn't an alien?"

I wasn't sure. I had been known to imagine that I was not *of* my mother the way most children were, that we had never been connected by the twisted, umbilical cord—my infant body tethered to her like a water lily to a murky pond. You could say that for some time now, I had been troubled by the notion of daughter as derivation (*d-e-r-i-v-a-t-i-o-n*). I had even tried to write this in a poem once, but my teacher said that poems were meant to be uplifting, "to instruct and delight," and all my poem did for the reader was make her feel like I needed a good psychiatrist.

"Come to my room," April says. "I have to show you something."

We close the door behind us and perch on her bed. Kelly is breeding rats in the basement, and April's dad is working at the city dump. Her mother, whom I adore, works the afternoon shift at Target and won't be home for several hours.

"Why so secretive?" I ask.

"This is a whopper. We can't take any chances with it."

From under her bed, April withdraws a copy of a book, what looks to be an old encyclopedia discontinued from her school's library. There is even a bold red DISCARDED stamp on the inside cover.

"Did you steal this?" I am so impressed my eyes gleam in the narrow light between the half-drawn curtains.

"Of course not. I just took it from the donations pile."

"Why?"

"It's a 'V,'" April tells me, arching her brows to imply something without actually saying it. "*As in—*"

"Oh, right." We share some vexing questions about our own anatomy.

"It turns out," she says, taking a slow, deep breath, "that there's this folk tale about—"

"What? You're killing me. What?"

"Teeth."

"Teeth?"

"Growing teeth. *Down there.*"

"Well, if it's a folk tale . . ."

"No, it can actually happen. It's rare, but it is possible that a certain kind of cyst can develop in a woman's—you know—" we still aren't brave enough to say the word—"and then she'll grow a second set of teeth. Think about it," April says, making her nauseous (*n-a-u-s-e-o-u-s*) face. "Where there are lips, it makes sense there are teeth."

"I'm not crazy about this second-mouth theory," I say. "I need to see what the entry says."

"There's a picture," April warns. "It's artsy, but still."

Softly, I read aloud, safe inside the boundaries of quotation marks: "The *vagina dentata,* Latin for 'toothed vagina,' describes the folklore in which a woman's vagina is said to contain teeth, implying that sexual intercourse with her is dangerous and might result in castration for her lover."

My mouth turns instantly dry, which amplifies the sound of each swallow. "I'll get the chocolate milk," April says.

What you know now is that your body will betray you. It is only a matter of time. First, there was the sweat, the new oils in your skin; now the blood that appears from the secret orifice. You realize that some words are harder to say because they are not meant to be spoken. You realize you admire other women's bodies as much as you fear your own. This is something else you were never intended to say, so you don't. There is a transformation that happens to some girls. It is only discussed in metaphor: the ugly duckling that becomes a swan, the gangly weed that blossoms into a flower. But these metaphors are lazy ones. You can barely tolerate their imprecision. Hasn't anyone noticed that a duck and a swan are not the same species? Neither is a weed simply another form of flower. Whatever happens that makes you a woman at last, it can be no less terrifying than birth, and worse because you are likely to remember it. Though now, when you think of being born, you will imagine the tunnel toothed and ridged, like pictures of stalagmite and stalactite you once saw in a special called "The Secret Life of Caves."

My mother kneels beside the bathtub and turns the hourglass upside down. "This is how long you have before I come back to wash your hair." I sit on the toilet seat cozy with my legs crossed, my body hunched around a towel.

"So are you going to get into the tub, or aren't you?" She tests the water with her elbow like I am still a baby, then turns to look at me with one of her most formidable (*f-o-r-m-i-d-a-b-l-e*) scowls.

"I will," I say—"after you go."

There is always this stand-off between us now, my blue eyes and her blue eyes locked together in a masterful vise.

"Whatever you're hiding," she snaps, "I'm going to find out anyway. Privacy is just as impermanent as anything else."

My mother regards me once more, shakes her head, then slams the door on her way into the hall.

Slowly, I unravel the coil of my torso and descend into the bubbly heat. Beneath the crumple of my clothes, I reach down and find my father's tin of Barbasol and one of his thin, terse razors purchased at the Dollar Store. Through the wall, I can hear them both, my parents, washing dishes and sweeping the kitchen floor. It is my mother who complains, my father who concurs, and I can hear this without knowing the actual words they speak. There is a rhythm to these after-dinner conversations that I keep time to; I hardly need the hourglass at all.

"So, you're really going to do it?" Kellie asks, taking my place on the toilet seat.

"Yup." I push my heels into the tiled wall and raise my legs up above the water. I begin to coat them with shaving cream while my sister watches. I don't mind if she sees, and I know she will never tell our mother.

"Don't you wish you had some instructions?" Kellie inquires. "I'm sure we could find some—in a book somewhere."

"How hard can it be?" I retort. "Really stupid girls at school shave their legs every day, and I'm already reading at an adult level."

"I doubt one has much to do with the other." Leave it to Kellie to start sounding like a professor at just this moment. Sometimes I can barely stand her—my sister, that hopeless pontificator (*p-o-n-t-i-f-i-c-a-t-o-r*).

"I don't want to discuss it," I tell her. "Let's talk about something else."

"What?"

I slide the plastic safety from the razor and watch it float away on the foam. "Marilyn Munster."

"OK. Why her?"

"Well, I think about her a lot." Kellie frowns at me. "Not *that way.* I think about how her aunt and uncle—they loved her, but they couldn't see her, not for who she really was. They just thought she was an ugly, hopeless freak." The razor makes a funny sound against my skin, like the one-armed paper cutter at school slicing through a stack of dittoes—one perfectly Xeroxed (*X-e-r-o-x-e-d*) ream. "But we, the audience—we know she isn't that at all. We know that, when it comes right down to it, *they're* the ugly, hopeless freaks."

"That's a little harsh, don't you think?"

"Don't get me wrong. I like Lily and Herman as much as the next person does, but they're the ones who aren't normal. They just *think* it's Marilyn who isn't."

"What does that have to do with anything?" Kellie wants to know.

"Perception," I say. "The truth has more to do with who's watching than with what's real."

For a moment, I feel proud of myself, proud of my big mind and my long legs in their state of transformation. I swoon with pride, leaning back against the soft shell pillow, watching the hair disappear from my legs. Then, suddenly, I feel the razor stick. I see the blood gushing out into the water before I even feel the sting, which is before I see the piece of flesh caught in the razor's teeth, the divot I've cut out of my skin.

The pain is sharp and high frequency, like someone striking a key at the very top of a piano. I try to wrap a washcloth around the wound, but the blood keeps seeping through, and I am wincing and writhing with only one smooth leg, the other wet with matted gold hairs.

Kellie is silent, and soon our mother's hand is on the knob, the door creaking open. "Time's up!" she calls, and sure enough, the hourglass sits helpless on the ledge, its belly full of bright white sand.

⧗

There were moments in your early life when you had intended to be a better sort of girl. At the very least, a different sort of girl from the girl you had become. Only some of it was physical. You could tell yourself all you wanted about that other world where families like the Munsters lived. In that world, on Mockingbird Lane, everyone drove hearses and kept gargoyles in their living rooms. They all had acne and wore glasses and left perspiration stains in their clothes. Their legs were all scarred from shaving accidents, which everyone considered a rite of passage. In your heart, though, you knew it wasn't true. The Munsters were one of a kind, and they were the wrong kind; it was only their oblivion that kept them safe, and you had lost yours the way you had lost every last one of your baby teeth. The new teeth were not deciduous. There would never be another chance. This was hard to admit, but you had to: You were not even Marilyn Munster, misplaced and misjudged, long-suffering in your loneliness and perfect beauty. Everyone had been right about you all along. You bite your tongue and clamp it tight to hold back tears. You are the monster in your own closet.

PART III

WHAT DOES IT MEAN TO HAVE A BODY?

Once upon a time, there was a young woman named after an angel. She was long and lithe with delicate features, able to balance without wobbling on the single blade of her skate. Each day after school, Celeste could be seen floating backwards with her leg extended as though through a heavenly ether, or pirouetting like a ballerina several inches above the smooth, white ice. Celeste wanted to skate in the Olympics one day, and she told her parents this was her solitary dream. Her coaches advised them to take out a loan and send the poised and elegant figure skater to Paris for further training.

Celeste was the older sister, Sabrina the younger. Sabrina had a brilliant mind but an ordinary body. No one knew if Celeste had a brilliant mind or not, since visible beauties have a way of eclipsing other kinds. Their father began working overtime. Sabrina began studying on her own, as they could no longer afford the tutor for her advanced work in math. And the young and promising Celeste was sent to Paris on a cloud. At home, their mother cooked and cleaned, just as she always had, but now she spent more time speaking of her daughter, *the Ice Skater,* peppering the walls with pictures of Celeste in her shimmery, sequined best.

In the summer, they all gathered at the airport to welcome her home from a year abroad. These were the old days, when families still stood at the gate and pressed their faces to the glass. They could see her coming up the ramp, or at least it was her teal suitcase bobbing along beside her. *Was this Celeste? Surely it couldn't be!* When she stepped into the light, her mother gasped. She was all flesh now. She had tried to disguise her new body with fabric waterfalls—the loose, wide-legged pants, the soft tunic slipping from her shoulder. The bone of that shoulder no longer pointed skyward like the hanger meant to hold her clothes in place. Even her neck was thick, so the cross she wore at her throat constricted against it—a choker now, a pendant no longer.

Celeste, seeing her mother, began to weep. "I'm finished," she murmured. "It was France. It was perfect. I loved the bakeries, all the fresh bread and cheese . . ."

They stood and cried together a long time while her father and sister looked on, silent. The next morning, the walls of the house were white and spare again, and Celeste's mother asked her father to please putty the holes where each of the nails had been.

⧗

It is easy to forget that Cinderella was once a ragamuffin of a girl, doing hard day labor in her stepmother's house. I always remember her as the princess-to-be, waltzing with Prince Charming in that dazzling blue gown. But when he comes to find her after the ball—in some versions, it is his messenger he sends—the girl is ordinary again: dirt on her face, a plain shift on her body. So ordinary is the Ash Girl in fact that they laugh at the mere suggestion *she* of all people should slip her commoner's foot into such a nice, regal shoe.

And so it is with Annabel Andrews. My mother says, "To think she grew up to be Jodie Foster, *the* Jodie Foster!" But wasn't she Jodie Foster even then, at thirteen, with her stringy blond hair and her low alto voice and her braces? I liked the look of her at the coffee shop, in the classroom, out on the hockey field. She had dirt on her face, a plain uniform on her body . . . Maybe I would have liked Cinderella, too—the preteen before the princess—shaking out rugs on the back porch, whistling as she hung a row of white shirts on the line.

The message seems to be that beauty takes time, that you're always better after than before. I know we're supposed to like the new Annabel better than the old, sans braces, with curls in her hair and perfectly manicured nails. A denim jumpsuit is just the '70s version of a ball gown after all. But it is also easy to forget that Annabel was her mother when all these changes occurred. Maybe Cinderella was also written by a mom, dedicated to a "tomboy teenaged daughter" in a state of pending reform.

"If we traded bodies," I ask my mother, "what's the first thing you'd do?"

She laughs a little, then shakes her head. "Oh, Julie, don't even get me started."

HOW DOES THE BODY DIFFER FROM A STORY?

Mrs. Sproul was Jennifer's mother. She had dark hair and dark eyes and dark skin the way Jennifer did, and I liked how you could see the veins winding up through her arms like ropes. When she came to visit us on Bring Your Mother to School day, she wore a shirt without any sleeves that looked like a blanket you'd drape over the back of a couch. Her head poked through in the middle, and her shiny hair was woven into a single, perfect braid.

"Did you help?" I ask Jennifer.

"No. My mother braids it herself."

Mrs. Sproul talks about what it means to be Native American. This confuses me because I thought we were all Native Americans unless we were born somewhere else. Then, she gives us cooked seaweed for snack, which isn't nearly as good as the homemade ice cream sandwiches my own mother made. It is salty, though, and I like Mrs. Sproul, so I ask for second helpings with extra rice to conceal the taste.

Then, Mrs. Sproul disappears. We don't see her standing in line with the other mothers, waiting for Jennifer after class. My mother says that Mrs. Sproul is sad because she was going to have a baby, but she lost it. *Did she put up pictures on a telephone pole? Had she checked with Audrey at the Lost and Found?* But it isn't like that, my mother says. The baby wasn't even born yet. The baby wasn't even fully formed.

How did she know it was there then? How can you lose something you haven't even had?

My mother says it is like a promise. Her body promised her a baby, but then, for reasons we don't understand, the promise was broken. Her body reneged, and Mrs. Sproul was betrayed. Just the thought of this—of Mrs. Sproul and her emptiness—flusters me, so my cheeks scorch and my heart floats up in my ears.

I earn a dollar every week as my allowance. I think how this money is promised to me, but what if my father, without explanation, decided to keep it instead? What if he never opened the top bureau drawer or fished out the rumpled bill from deep in his trouser pocket?

It wouldn't be any less of a loss, would it, than if I had dropped the dollar myself through one of those grates on a busy street?

⧗

There is a new show on television called *Beverly Hills 90210*. My mother believes it is a family show like *Highway to Heaven*. My mother is mistaken. We make popcorn and pour Shasta into plastic cups. There is a white board on a tripod left out from Win, Lose, or Draw, which we will use if it becomes necessary to visualize anything.

"From what I've read," my mother says, "this first episode of the new season is going to talk about pregnancy. Your father and I feel that we need to address this subject as well."

"But you can't have any more children," I say.

"This isn't about *us*," my father replies. "This is about *you*."

"Me?"

"You're about to start seventh grade." *Had he always had such bushy eyebrows, such serious eyes?* "I think we all know what that means."

Brenda has thick, dark hair with blunt-cut bangs and full, pouty lips. She has a twin brother named Brandon, a wealthy boyfriend named Dylan, and she is terrified that she is pregnant. In the end, it turns out she isn't pregnant, but she does learn a valuable lesson about how dangerous it is to be a girl.

When the episode is over, my mother peers into my face and inquires, "Do you know what it was that Brenda did that made her think she was pregnant?"

I nod my head.

"Can you explain it to us?"

When I don't respond, my mother reaches for a marker.

"Please don't draw that big cow's head," I plead, which is how the diagram of the female reproductive system always looks to me.

"Julie, we need to know that you're following what we're trying to teach you here." My father wipes his mouth and sits up straighter in his chair. "Sex doesn't just determine what happens to you in the afterlife; it's about the way your whole future could be destroyed in *this* life."

I nod again, wipe my moist hands on the sofa cushions.

"I'll put it as plain as I know how," my mother says. "This is you now," and she draws a stick figure with a big head of permed hair at one end of the white board. Then, she draws a line to the other end and puts the same permed stick figure holding hands with a plain stick figure. "This is you twenty years from now when you're married." She adds two small stick figures beside the plain stick figure and me. "You and your husband will have children," which is another (nicer) way of saying that my husband and I will have sex. I don't want to think about this, but now I must. I see a penis like a party snake in the middle of the cow's head diagram in my mind.

"Sometime soon," my mother says, drawing a downward-facing arrow to an early point on the line, "you will get your period." I wince as though I have been pierced by that same arrow. "The time between your period and your marriage—" she picks up a red marker now and shades the line furiously from the dot to the plain stick figure—"is the most perilous time of your life."

"There are going to be temptations," my father says, but thankfully, he doesn't contribute anything to my mother's illustration.

"The question is, Julie, what are you going to do with these next twenty years?"

I open my mouth, but it is dry, empty of words and ideas.

"What are you *not* going to do?" my father prods.

"Sex?" I squeak.

"Good. But say it like you mean it."

"And with all the time that you're not having sex," my mother says, capping her marker at last, "you'll be avoiding pregnancy *and* going to medical school."

My father smiles at me now, his jaw unclenched. "Think what a success you will be!"

WHAT IS THE BODY IF NOT ALSO A METAPHOR?

We all know Pollyanna had it coming to her. She was cheerful and kind and talked to everyone in her charming English way, but she also questioned authority and broke a series of rules, including Aunt Polly's curfew and insistence she stay at home during the Fourth of July picnic.

I knew about corporal punishment, but this was different. No one spanked Pollyanna for sneaking out of the house and climbing down the tree. The situation was worse than that. Pollyanna was punished physically in a way that made it seem like she had punished herself. Maybe God did it—made her fall so she would be lame and have to travel away on a train to get leg surgery. That's a pretty powerful wake-up call about what can happen if you don't do as you're told. Or maybe it wasn't God, just the writer showing us instead of telling us that you can't get away with things—that there are no actions without consequences.

I wonder if she had been climbing that tree to rescue a kitten or because the house was on fire and there was no other escape—would she have fallen? Somehow I think God (or the writer) would have spared her. But it was her vanity—the fact that she wanted to be seen as the solo in the singing flag—that caused her to lose the use of her legs.

This was the problem with punishment. It always seemed like a simple hole in the wall, a crack in the plaster of your best intentions. But when you climbed into that hole, or were pushed through, you saw there was a whole room behind it, and sometimes this room was draughty and dank, unsettled all the way to its very foundations.

⧗

Janine looked a little like Hayley Mills after she grew up and played the principal on *Saved by the Bell.* She told me a story once about her affair with a man who drove a black Porsche and was married to another woman.

"I was lonely," she said, "single and lonely. I knew it was wrong, but I think I kind of liked that it was wrong. Does that make sense?"

We sat together in the break room at work. I ate my sandwich quietly and in a way that made her feel she could tell me anything, even though I was young and a virgin and had only seen Porsches in James Bond movies.

"Anyway, I liked to be seen riding around in that Porsche with him. I felt like the chosen one, even if it was only on certain afternoons. I liked how he would have the men valet-park it when we went to restaurants and hotels, and they would look at me like I was somebody special—his wife maybe."

She paused to lift her Lean Cuisine out of the microwave.

"But good things—that are really bad things—always come to an end. We were driving on this road with beautiful scenery but a lot of sharp turns, and he was driving too fast, of course, because what's the point of having a Porsche if you don't drive too fast? It was summer, so the sun roof was open, and he took a corner so fast that we collided with another car, and I was launched out of the Porsche through the roof like a catapult. I don't know much about physics, but I'm pretty sure it was a one-in-a-million chance. I broke my neck, he went back to his wife, and we never saw each other again."

"But I thought, if you broke your neck—"

She finishes my sentence for me—"that you died? Automatically? Well, you don't. Not always. I was in the hospital a long time, and eventually, they made this suit for me that helped to fuse my head back onto my body. I went around looking like a member of a bomb squad. I'd stand in supermarket checkout lines, and everybody would stare at me silently. I didn't feel human anymore. I wasn't sure I wanted to survive."

For my part, I wasn't sure why Janine was telling me this story. We chewed in silence for a while, and I glanced at her neck a few times, trying to pry behind her collar with my eyes. Then, she was paged to the selling floor, so she stood up (*was she always so stiff? why had I never noticed before?)* and tossed her lunch in the trash.

"Whatever you do," Janine said, looking fondly at me, and wistful, too, "just remember that no fuck is worth all that."

WHY DOES THE BODY SPEAK A RIDDLED LANGUAGE?

The Bemis family is not invested in beautiful things or in what people think of their belongings. Neither are they interested in what people think of their bodies, even though *your body,* my mother repeats, her tongue stuck like a record needle, *is beyond a doubt your most valuable possession.*

I beg my mother to let me stay with Shannon while she is away marking prices on masking tape squares for the annual church rummage sale. "What will you do there?" she asks. "I find it hard to believe such a pig sty could be an enticing place to play."

Shannon has painted a rainbow on her bedroom wall, the arc of it spanning the headboard of her large, unmade, grown-up bed. We are allowed to jump on that bed, and outside on the giant trampoline. We are allowed to take cushions from the furniture and pile them up at the foot of the stairs and practice leaping from higher and higher levels until we are like Superman, nearly horizontal in the air.

But when we arrive at the Bemis house, there is an ambulance wailing away, and one of the neighbors stands out in her yard with Shannon's brother, one hand on his back and a broom in the crook of her elbow.

"Are you the Wades?" she asks. "Doris wanted me to wait on you."

"What was the ambulance doing here?" I demand.

"Well, dear, it's a crying shame. You know, Shannon has such a severe allergy. Deathly one it can be. I saw it out my kitchen window, saw her turning breathless and blue, so I made the 9-1-1 call. She was dancing in the grass, the way children do, and with her bare foot, she stepped right on one—a hornet, I think they said."

I look down at the tight huarache sandals I'm not allowed to take off, think of the stripes they leave on my skin—half white, half tan.

Daniel scratches his greasy head. "I dared her to do it. It's all my fault."

"Now hush, honey," the neighbor says. She wears a bright red kerchief with bobby pins holding her stray hairs in. To my mother, she murmurs, "Can you imagine not being able to run barefoot in your own backyard?"

⧗

Some men are very fond of my mother. Al Kalamar is one of them. She enjoys the attention and always says, with a wry laugh that makes my father nervous: "They can look, but they can't touch. Touching costs extra."

The men tend to be old; often, they are widowed. They like the idea of a woman who knows how to take charge of things. There is my mother down on her knees, fighting the weeds like a ruthless, advancing army. "It's so hard," she laments, "to have anything nice in this world."

I picture the green sprigs with loaded machine guns, coming to take her flowers hostage.

Then, Al Kalamar appears. He lives two houses away, but when you are old, this is a long walk on legs that creak like rusty hinges. He blends in with the surroundings at first: dark green pants, dark brown shirt, flannel even in summer.

"Planting anything new?" he asks. Or: "How are those azaleas doing?" It's always a question with an obvious answer, but my father says he's harmless, lonely, just looking for someone to talk to.

"Why is his nose so big?" I say. "And why does it look like a tomato?"

My father and I gather vagrant blossoms from the shedding camellia tree. "He has a little problem with alcohol, Smidge. It isn't polite to talk about it."

I think on this a while, how a secret love of drink can show in the nose, can display in such a way that it is no longer secret.

"What about his pants?" I ask.

"What about them?"

"Why do they point straight out at the zipper whenever Mom is around? Sometimes they look like an elevator, going up and down."

IS THE BODY DESTINED TO BE LONELY?

Once upon a time, there was a young woman named Liesl who loved to sneak out of the house after supper and dance in the gazebo. She was in love, or falling in love, with a young man named Rolfe who delivered telegrams to her father. On their own, both were average-looking people, but more interesting than average because they were European. When they danced together, especially inside the gazebo during a lightning-and-thunder storm, they became beautiful, radiant. Their movements were smooth and synchronized. They fit together like a teacup and saucer.

But love is never easy. The summer storm is also a metaphor. Someone always has a curfew, or pricks her finger on a spinning wheel, or gets her braces caught in someone else's hair. Liesl might have fallen the way Pollyanna did, crawling in through the high window, having just kissed a soon-to-be Nazi in the rain. *There has to be a consequence for this.* But as it is, her dress is stained, and the new governess agrees to keep her secret for her, to lend her a towel and a clean nightgown and even talk with her awhile. The governess is also a nun, which means she must remain neutral in romantic terms, and she must never let a man sweep her off her feet, let alone waltz her to Rogers & Hammerstein.

Except the new governess is also in love, or falling in love, with Liesl's father, the master of the house who was once a captain in the navy but is now a widower with seven children to raise. *Is she more attracted to his power or to his vulnerability?* This is hard to say. But then the Baroness arrives from her castle in Vienna, and she is more beautiful than anyone else in the room. Or any room. Her hair is white-gold, and her gown is white-gold, and even the Champagne in her glass is white-gold. They will dance, the Captain and the Baroness, and everyone will agree that they look well together. The Captain will also never be a Nazi, which adds more points in his favor.

But then the governess breaks the cardinal rule about nuns dancing, and she blushes in the captain's arms. *There has to be a consequence for this.* So she flees, back to the abbey where she makes a silent vow and refuses to come out of her room. This is because she knows, in her innermost heart, that she would throw Jesus over in a second for one night in a gazebo with that man.

Is there a lesson here? Is there a moral?

Maybe: Love's most familiar form is a triangle. (Liesl + Rolfe + Hitler; The Governess + The Captain + The Baroness; alt. The Governess + The Captain + The Holy Savior.)

Or: The most beautiful one is not always the most satisfied one. (Think of the Baroness, awash in beauty like a night in the rain, slinking off to her castle alone.)

Or: To dance is to enter a hot kiln, to fire the soft pot of the heart into something solid. (That which can only keep or break. That which can never bend.)

⧗

Love looks different after World War II and Vietnam and the Cold War. Love looks different in America, too. If you were raised on fairy tales, you might not recognize love at first in the fluorescent American light of the roller rink or the bowling alley. You might not recognize love in the sticky-sweet of the blue raspberry Icee, the stale scent of the snack bar, with its popcorn and corn dogs, its nachos with extra cheese, *American* cheese, pumped from a tub shaped like a soap dispenser. Love is a casual excess here, like Good & Plenty at the movies (*that bottomless box!*), or a bright distraction, like the disco ball that strobes across the skating floor or dangles above the newly waxed lane.

We were learning how to double date. We were learning how to turn love from a triangle into two sets of boxed seats, a booth at the diner where one boy and one girl sit on each side. A mirror image. A microcosm of the larger world of mothers and fathers on benches at barbecues.

"It just makes sense," April says from the bathroom stall beside mine. "Everything else comes in pairs. Think about salt and pepper shakers." She had a point there. "Don't you see how it's bound to happen? I mean"—flushing now—"you can't take love off the table."

There was no gazebo at the roller rink. We only had the pay phone with the broken cord and the pinball machine that sometimes lit up for no reason. Even if there had been a lightning-and-thunder storm, no one could have heard it above the roar of so many Riedell wheels and the DJ playing Celine Dion at full volume. This was long before she knew her heart would go on, long before any of us did. *But how do you cross that gap, like a sidewalk crack, between the last Before and the first After?*

Lee takes my sweaty palm in his sweaty palm. It's "Beauty and the Beast" now, from the new Disney film. The lights are dimmed for a couples' skate. "COUPLES ONLY!" the DJ commands, so all the singles have to clear the floor through breaks in the carpeted wall. There is a certain shame in this, a skulking off into shadows, a defeated return to the soda fountain. Lee and I are in the rotation now, the record of love that spins round and round, and that's when we see them: off in the distance, incandescent, beside the vending machine with its deep green glow. They are leaning against the wall: Julie Winder with her white-gold hair, Michael Shields with his white-gold hair, their pale bodies pressing into each other, bubbling like Champagne they've never tasted, their sticky-sweet mouths careening out of control.

Ever just the same, ever a surprise . . . Our fingers part on the curve . . . "Sorry!" I shout to Lee over my shoulder. "I have to go to the bathroom again."

WHY SHOULD WE HAVE BODIES, AS OPPOSED TO SOMETHING ELSE?

Mr. Reid is retiring. This is all I know. He and his wife are hosting a party at an expensive hotel with fountains in the lobby and an aquarium with scores of exotic fish.

"I thought those were only for doctors' offices," I whisper to my mother, whose lips are pursed, whose eyes are narrowed on my body.

"Is this dress getting snug?" she asks, tugging hard at the waist. "It's costly to have another growth spurt, but I'd rather you were growing *up* than *out.*"

"I guess James Bond had an aquarium in his bedroom—"

"Stop mumbling to yourself and stand up straight!" she insists. "Now remember that there are a lot of important people in there, including the editor from *The West Seattle Herald.* Mrs. Reid has assured me she can introduce you, which might be a nice way for you to advance in the world of journalism."

I don't remind her that I'm only twelve, as new to my number as I am to the heels of my shoes, the paint on my mouth, the first mascara thick on my lashes. It is not waterproof either—that is a lie—and I should know because I have been crying often since Lee Bennett left me for Marissa Sheldon.

Inside the grand parlor where the party is held, I am soon separated from my parents and left to graze the buffet table alone.

"The salmon's quite delicious, if I do say so myself," decrees a dapper old man in an argyle sweater vest. "I believe it's poached, and the seasoning is divine."

I smile at him, as his words have given me permission to shovel a hearty helping of pink fish onto my plate.

"Ah," he nods. "I admire a woman of robust appetite."

I glance around just to be sure that I am the intended subject of this conversation. "How rude of me not to introduce myself!" the man resumes, extending a speckled hand. "I'm Timothy Reid."

"Oh," I sigh, "this is *your* party. Happy retirement, Mr. Reid!"

He laughs and mutters *delightful, just delightful* under his breath. "No need for such formality, then. Call me Timmy."

"Timmy?"

"Yes. And you are . . . Miss—?"

"*Julie,*" I say, hoping for a pause during which I can cram some salmon into my mouth.

"First-name basis already! Lovely, my dear. Now I presume you're here with a young man? Who is the lucky son of a gun?"

My eyes convey my surprise, and I shake my head while chewing the salmon as fast as I can.

"Blasphemy!" Mr. Reid exclaims. "Am I to infer that a woman of such desirable attributes is . . . dare I say it . . . *unattached*?"

"I had a boyfriend," I reply, and before I can reach for the punch, he hands me a glass of wine. "It didn't work out, though."

"And where did you meet this foolish fellow who allowed you to slip away?" Mr. Reid's hand rests lightly on my elbow, and he stares deeply into my eyes. *Who knew grown-ups could care so much about a preadolescent girl's problems?*

"At school," I say. "It's the only place I really meet anybody, but then he met somebody else."

"Of course! I should have guessed you were a career-track girl. Too smart not to be. Do you go to State or University?"

"I go to Calvary Lutheran now," I say, "but I used to go to West Seattle Christian."

"Small colleges, are they? For teachers and nurses, that sort of thing?"

"Oh, they're not *colleges,*" I tell him, fighting the urge to laugh. "I'm just starting seventh grade. And, while I appreciate you being so friendly and all, I don't really think I can drink your wine."

I hand the glass back to him, Mr. Reid, *Timmy,* in the argyle sweater vest, whose face is falling faster now than a flower left too long in the vase.

⧗

Then, all at once, I am older. It is the new millennium—in London, no less—prolepsis of speed and light and faraway places. I have left the country of my birth, but the curls of my childhood traveled with me. They are false curls, achieved with a kit and chemicals, curls I long to shed like weighty camellia blossoms.

"What can I do for you, love?" the woman inquires, stepping outside the salon for a smoke.

"These curls," I say. "What would you recommend for me instead?"

"American?" she asks.

I nod.

"Study abroad?"

I nod again.

"What are you—twenty, twenty-one?"

"Twenty," I say. It is the oldest I have ever been, simple and obvious, but it is also the oldest I have ever imagined being. The years begin to grow in thick now, dark and dense, profuse as the Coke can curls my mother still perms over her kitchen sink.

The woman takes a quick drag, looks up and down the street as though we are under surveillance, then waves me inside. "Rescue mission," she says to the other stylist.

"Well, for what it's worth, I think your curls are *adorable*." She is sweeping up around her station while one foot keeps time to the radio.

"Thanks," I say. "Problem is, from behind you can't tell if I'm fifty-five, or ten and tall for my age."

"Right. Have a seat for me here. Lucy, would you bring us each a cuppa?"

"What do I look like then? Your servant?"

"More like my sister. Do it before you're disowned."

They exchange birds on matching, manicured fingers before Lucy grins and sets to work making tea on the electric kettle.

"So, we're going to take off some of these ringlets."

"*All* of them," I reply with new conviction.

"And you want to go short, I wager?"

"As short as my face will allow."

"We can do it," she says, squinting at me in the mirror. "I feel it's only fair to warn you, though: people are sensitive to haircuts. Have you ever worn your hair short before?"

"Not super short, no. But I'm not worried about it. I'm looking to make a new start."

"On the lam, are you? Running from the law and all that?" I smile and shake my head. "Didn't figure you were the type . . ."

She wets her comb and begins the slow process of disentanglement. "Are you running from a romance gone wrong?"

"More than one," I murmur.

"Back in the States, I take it?"

"I needed some distance," I say. "Sometimes an ocean helps."

"I'm going to take this short, *really* short. You have the cheekbones for it." The kettle whining in the background now. "You're going to see your curls piling up on the floor like a mountain of girly-girl, and it's not going to faze you one bit. Am I right then?"

"Right."

"Tea. Do you take it black or white?"

"Milk and sugar," I say to Lucy. "Thank you."

"And in the States," the woman says, working harder now, feeling the curls resist her, resist being unsnarled, "was it men you were dating then?"

Our eyes meet in the mirror. My arm hairs begin to bristle under the plastic gown. "Yes. *Of course.*"

"Right. Quite right."

When she doesn't continue with this line of questions, I press her: "Why did you ask about men before?"

Lucy sets the teacup down on the counter. "Careful, it's hot," she warns.

"No reason. Just curious."

"Do I look—is there something—?" A warm panic moves through me like a wave.

"No, not at all. It's only that, every once and a while, a woman will say, 'When you cut my hair that way, I'm mistaken for a lesbian.'"

WHAT IF SUDDENLY, AFTER A LONG LAPSE IN MEMORY, THE BODY REMEMBERS?

Once upon a time, there were two teenaged girls named Deanna and Heidi. They were both only children and had been friends since first grade. Often, they were mistaken for sisters, even though they lacked any physical resemblance. Deanna was tall with bronze skin and brown eyes and strong muscles in her arms from years of playing tennis and basketball. Heidi was short with yellow hair and pale skin and a few vexing freckles that made her look younger than she was. Afternoons, it was common to see them walking together through the waterfront neighborhood.

In high school, Deanna had a steady boyfriend, and Heidi went out on dates with a number of eligible boys. Deanna's mother had been known to remark that her daughter often flirted shamelessly to get something she wanted—a discount at the ice cream shop, a refund without a receipt at the mall. Dunja recounted these episodes with a tone of mock annoyance, as if, beyond her initial outrage that her daughter batted her eyes and swung her hips in pursuit of special treatment, she was also relieved to see such feminine behaviors. "She's all girl," Dunja would sigh, "which means she's nothing but trouble."

One afternoon, Deanna's parents returned to a quiet house. They were used to the girls sprawled out on the living room rug, drinking sodas through licorice straws and laughing at something on television.

"Will you bring me some fried onions for the casserole?" Dunja asked her husband. Before he could reply, she recited: "Downstairs, pantry, third shelf on the right."

Ivo nodded, wanting only to collapse in his recliner chair, but knowing better than to say this to his wife.

In the basement, he noticed the light bulb with the dangling string aglow in the corner of the room. Dunja wouldn't like that, he thought, and the last thing he needed was one of her lectures on the cost of electricity. He switched off the light. But then, on his way to the pantry, he saw another light, beaming from under the laundry room door. He would have to speak to Deanna about this, but privately, to protect her from her mother's temper.

Ivo opened the door. Everything happened like a movie montage: a series of swift jump cuts and then the camera's slow, panoramic sweep as he averted his eyes, twisted his body away. His daughter, Deanna. Her back exposed. Her shirt on the floor. Heidi perched on the washing machine. Her legs wrapped around Deanna's waist, pulling her in, pulling her close. Nothing accidental about the posture. The deep, fraught kisses. The hands lost in each other's hair.

⧗

"At least Joyce has two daughters," my mother remarks. "I wasn't so lucky. With you, there is no Plan B."

When I ask her what she means, she tells me to stop dilly-dallying and pull those nylons over my knees. "It's a wedding," she says. "Let's try to make ourselves presentable, shall we?"

"But what were you saying about Amy and Brenda before?"

"Linda, we're going to be late," my father calls from the hall. "Do you have any idea what the traffic is like on that side of town?"

"Give us five minutes," she snaps. "I still have a little magic to work," and sets about moussing my hair.

"It seems like I haven't seen Amy in forever. Is she—"

"God only knows," my mother sighs. "God only knows *where* she is and *what* she is doing. But whatever you do, don't ask Joyce or Ed about her. This is Brenda's big day, and the last thing they need is a slew of questions from nosy you."

"So Amy won't be there? She's the older sister. I figured she would be the maid of honor."

"As if any tradition was ever sacred to that girl!" Now my mother is scrunching and furiously picking my hair while studying her own complexion in the mirror.

"I won't ask any questions of them, but just between you and me—"

My mother exhales sharply. "Amy is in a cult! There, I've said it. Are you satisfied?"

I shake my head. "What do you mean, *a cult?*"

"Exactly what it sounds like. Some *Canadian* cult—in Manitoba or one of those other Godforsaken places. And she is married to a man who is *twice* her age!"

"Really?"

"Never let on to Joyce you know. She told me under the strictest confidence. Obviously, understandably, she's embarrassed." My mother leans down and whispers dramatically in my ear: "Amy *eloped* with this man—this *Canadian cult leader*—almost five years ago now. Can you imagine? What a disgrace! She calls them sometimes, but she won't come home. Joyce is terrified that she's going to have his baby, and then she'll never get away."

I haven't seen Amy in years, but I have to admit I'm surprised by her moxie. Moxie—or folly. It is hard to say. I never trust my mother to tell me the whole story.

When we arrive at the church, Joyce intercepts us in the narthex and draws my mother and me into the ladies' room. "Bill, go find a seat," my mother instructs, and I watch as he follows the stream of organ music toward the sanctuary.

"I'm a wreck," Joyce confides as soon as we are out of earshot.

"What is it? What's wrong? Did Amy—"

"No, it's Brenda. She's sick. Can you believe it? She is *sick* on her wedding day."

"You have been *beset* by misfortune," my mother concurs.

"And you know, Brenda is our good daughter. She and David have waited all this time. Now she's gotten on the Pill, and they're all ready for the big night, except she's sick, and the doctor says there could be some kind of interaction between the antibiotics and her birth control, so he wants them to use a different kind of contraception." Joyce's neck strains against her doily collar. "As a *precaution.*"

I turn my eyes down to the pink tile floor, the grout between the pink tiles, the dirt in the grout between the pink tiles.

"Condoms?" my mother murmurs, in the same tone she uses for phrases like *tax audit* and *devil in disguise.*

"Well, David's not having anything to do with it. They've had a big fight, and—who can blame him?—he says to her, 'I haven't waited two years to have sex with my wife only to be told I have to wear a rubber.'"

"So, she'll just risk it? Or will she get involved with a diaphragm and all that business?"

I can't believe what I'm hearing, and my eyes dart up from the floor, gauge the seriousness of their expressions, start to turn away. "She's sick!" I say, turning back. "What if she doesn't feel like having sex? Why should she have to?"

Joyce opens her mouth to speak, but no sound comes out, and my mother's eyebrows furrow deeply, letting me know that I have crossed a line for which there will be consequences. "Julie, this is really no concern of yours. You can't possibly understand—"

"It isn't rocket science," I say. "When I'm sick, I don't even want to get off the couch. I don't feel like doing anything, let alone having someone paw all over me, stick his—"

Now Joyce brings her hand to her heart like she is about to recite the Pledge of Allegiance. "*Julie! Enough!*" my mother barks. "Have some respect. It's their wedding night, and a man has a right to expect certain things from his wife on their wedding night."

WHAT IF THE BODY BECOMES ITS OWN ADVERSARY?

At the college dorm, Christmas lights glow year-round—in the parlors, around the doorframes, along the check-in desk where the senior resident assistant is on duty till ten o'clock.

But it is after eleven now, and he has been kissing me every place we can think of—the park bench, the movie theater, the front seat of the borrowed car, and now the phone booth in the lobby, which is only ever used by girls with calling cards, girls trying to reach family overseas.

"I love phone booths," I whisper, as he closes the door behind us.

"Why phone booths?"

"Think about Clark Kent."

"I want to think about you." He presses his weight against me. He kisses me: my neck, my collarbones.

"The phone booth is a site of transformation," I insist.

It surprises me how much I like the close quarters, the heat our bodies make in the tight space. He is taller than I am, which is also a relief. It is not often I get to feel smaller than someone.

"Come upstairs with me," I say.

"Won't we get in trouble?"

"Becky's gone for the whole week, and the RA can sleep through anything."

He nods and follows me up the back stairs, our fingers interlaced, our breath still ragged from using our mouths so much. I love the feeling of being wanted like this, of inciting a verifiable physical response in him. He tells me I have beautiful hands and beautiful lips, two features of my body that I am proud of all on my own, without help from anyone. His compliment tells me he sees me as I see myself, which is more important even than seeing me as I want to be seen.

There are two rooms, the anteroom and the bedroom. I don't bother turning on the lights. The moon is bright, and the courtyard outside the window is dotted with old-fashioned lampposts and bright blue emergency phones. We make shadows against the wall, kissing our way toward the second threshold. I don't know what will happen, how far we will go. I am open to anything, everything, my heart a parachute splayed newly soft and wide.

His hands hold to my waist, wet with sweat. I lift them gently to my breasts, only to feel them fall away. We spin on our heels. We are breathless in the half-dark. I lift his hands, and he lowers them, anchored to my hips. When I try the third time, he parts his lips. "I can't do that," he says.

"What?"

"Touch you there."

"You can," I say. "It's OK. I'm giving you permission."

"It's not your permission I need," he replies, and I feel the distance in the lower half of his torso, his body pulling away.

"What do you mean? I *want* you to."

"But Jesus," he says. "Jesus doesn't."

⧗

"So, is it true love?" Becky asks, grinning at me across the cafeteria table.

"Not exactly."

"Well, it's the first time for both of you. That can be tricky. No one to take the lead."

"Oh, I took it, but he didn't follow."

"What do you mean?" Her eyes are so blue and full of concern, eyes I could never tire of looking into.

"It turns out that he has *boundaries*. Apparently, Jesus doesn't want him to do me."

"Oh my God!" She drops her head to the table with a thud.

"*Literally.* But it's not that. It's more than that. I don't really care that he won't touch my breasts. I don't even know what I like yet. But there's this whole difference-of-opinion-about-the-nature-of-the-world thing that bothers me."

"Because you're not a Christian, and he is." Becky looks at me, her cheeks rosy with atheist empathy.

"I don't know if I'm not . . . I mean, I was raised to be. I'm just—I'm not that strict about it. I'm—exploring my spiritual options."

"What did I say to you from the very beginning?"

"I know, I know."

"Do you think now, *maybe,* there might be some stock in it? I mean, people have used craftier excuses than Jesus to get out of sex before." Becky raises her white-gold eyebrows suggestively at me.

"Look. I don't know about that. I don't know about—his *preferences*—whatever. But it's like, the way my mom described it, there were supposed to be all these boys groping me all the time, feeding me these lines, trying to swindle me out of Christ's holy treasure—"

"Just to be clear: is that your virginity?"

"Oh, shut up!" I laugh in spite of myself. "But it hasn't been that way at all. I mean, I haven't had to peel them off like

Band-aids. My mother always said that women were the keepers of virtue, but every guy I meet makes me seem like *I'm* the villain."

"Well, *I'm* late for class," Becky says. "We'll have to talk about this tonight. But don't beat yourself up. Some things are more complicated than they seem. And I still think you might be dealing with a closet case."

"All right, all right. Duly noted."

I am walking behind her toward the exit doors: Becky, tall and lean, at least my height, maybe taller, her long, golden hair gleaming against her back. Then, I notice her ID card has fallen to the floor. I stoop to pick it up, call after her. She turns as if in slow motion: hair wrapping around her shoulder, hip jutting out to the side.

"Oh, thanks," she smiles, but her hands are full: one clasping the tray, the other her mug.

"I could slip it in your back pocket for you," I offer. It seems so harmless as I say it, just a simple gesture of help for a friend. But then I see the cloud glide across her clear eyes. Her face a painting now, a false mirror.

"That's OK," Becky says, pausing, holding me in her sightline. *Is it suspicion I see? I can't be sure.* "You can just hand it to me when we get outside."

WHEN THE BODY CALLS OUT, WHO OR WHAT WILL ANSWER?

At the bowling alley, my father says, "It's nice to see you," and I realize he is speaking to me.

"What do you mean, Dad? You see me all the time."

"Oh, it's just that we used to spend every weekend together when you were a kid, but now that you're older, I feel like we're only passing each other in the halls."

I smile at him, the parent I take after: quick to sentiment, slow to anger. I fan my hands over the cool air, look down to the end of the lane where the pins are swiftly restored to standing. "Do you want to play again?" I ask.

"Sure. Here," and he fishes out the bills from his wallet. "Go ahead and get us a couple of sodas, too. In just a few years, it'll be a couple of beers."

At the counter, I tell the man my lane and ask to purchase another game. "And while I'm at it," I say, "these shoes are a little big. Could I trade them in for a smaller size? Maybe an eight instead of a nine?"

The man chuckles, rubs the stubble under his chin. "Women and their shoe sizes. My wife's the same way."

"What do you mean?"

"Oh, she'd rather have them pinching her feet than admit she needs to go up a number."

"But these really are too loose," I say. "I can fit my whole thumb in the back of my heel."

"Sure, sure," he nods. "A size eight?" Then, appraising me over the counter: "That's a pretty small shoe for a woman like you."

"Excuse me?" I look around, half-expecting to see Dom Deluise lurking behind the plastic ferns. *Surprise! You're on Candid Camera!* Or maybe I am wishing for my kind, well-meaning father to rush indignantly to my side. *Just what exactly you are implying, sir?*

"No need to get all hot and bothered about it," the man sighs, holding the striped size eights out like a grudging peace offering. He winks at me as I take the shoes in my hand. "I can pretend as well as you can that a big, broad-shouldered gal walks around on a pair of dainty paws."

⧗

Autumn in Pike Place. The red and gold trees mingling with the pines. The mountain that seems to float across the Sound. Home again to my city of sea gulls and salty air, the pleasures of stout coffee and oversized turtleneck sweaters. Becky and April and I stroll through the Market together. I wonder how long I will live here, now that I've gone away. I wonder how long this here will live in me, once I'm gone for good. A city written into the body, embedded, like rock in a cliffside: there's something elemental there, indistinguishable from the cliff itself. *We are where we are from?* Parents? Places? I couldn't believe this was true. *We are not where we are not from?* Truer perhaps. Still not the whole story.

I browse through a batch of old records, even as I have long since given my record player away. Simon & Garfunkel. I hold them up, consider the sincerity in their grainy faces.

"So, have I told you how much I love your new hair?" Becky says.

"It looks amazing on you," April agrees. "I could never go that short, never in a million years."

"Oh, no, me neither, but it really suits her." They stand as a pair, united in opinion, admiring.

"Thanks, but stop. You're embarrassing me." I look down at the records again, and when I raise my eyes, I notice an old man with a pipe in his mouth, studying me across a crate of books. He resembles a weathered statue of a fisherman, so my mind cloaks him instantly in a yellow raincoat, the kind with the matching hood.

"Good day," he nods after a few moments pass. He turns his gaze to my friends, to me, and back again. "I cannot recall," the man says, in a voice raspy with tobacco and age, "when I have seen a more beautiful girl. Look at her," he insists, gesturing toward me. "Those eyes. That face. I could have sworn I'd died and gone to Heaven!"

PART IV

As a child in confirmation class, I am instructed in the holy math. "Seven is the number of completion," our pastor says. "It took seven days for God to make the world, so seven days became the length of our earthly week." He speaks to us as a single mass, the cloud and not the snowflakes, separate and unique.

"But you know that seven can be made by adding other numbers together. One and six. Two and five. From God's perspective, the most important of these are three and four." Pastor John writes 3+4=7 on the green chalkboard; I copy this problem on the first page of my standard-issue St. Paul's of Shorewood Lutheran Bible. "Three is a heavenly number," the pastor says. "God is especially partial to three because God exists in three forms. Who are the three members of the Trinity?"

"God the Father, God the Son, God the Holy Ghost," we recite in unison. No wonder he forgets we are not one person. (But we never forget that Now and Laters are at stake for our collective participation.)

"Good! Three represents Heaven, and four represents Earth. When you add them together, they equal All There Is."

Waving my hand, I ask, "Why is four the number for Earth?"

"Think about it," the pastor says. "There are four directions on the compass: north, south, east, west. There are four corners in a room. We have four limbs to balance our bodies—two arms and two legs. We even have four chambers in our hearts."

⧗

That now was then. This now is later. Every magazine I open, every screen I scroll down, makes similar promises: *Take this quiz to determine your contours. You'll get specific health, eating, and exercise advice, plus fashion tips to flatter your figure.* The human snowflake, it seems, also comes in four forms. *Using this science-based tool, reviewed by our experts, discover whether you are an apple, a spoon, a ruler, or an hourglass.* And all this time I had been thinking I was a woman.

In ninth grade, I start Catholic school where we buy our books instead of borrow. One of the sisters instructs me to stand in the far line by the window. "You'll need to purchase a Bible," she says.

"But I have a Bible, several Bibles. NIV, King James—"

"You're Protestant," she decrees. *How did she know? How could she tell?* If I protest, I will only confirm her claim. "At Holy Names, we require a Catholic Bible."

The first afternoon, outside on the lawn, I open my new Bible, compare it to the old. There are seven more books in the Catholic Old Testament—what we will come to call *Easter eggs* in the age of DVDs. For now, they are a bonus track at the end of a tape, extra footage after the final credits roll. I circle their titles: *Tobit, Judith, The Book of Wisdom, Sirach, Baruch, First Maccabees, Second Maccabees.* I will have to inquire about these tomorrow.

Sister Ann Cornelia is our school librarian. I figure she is the best one to ask, since her spiritual vocation and her earthly occupation both involve books—notably, the Bible.

"You're thinking like a Protestant," she says, hands folded on her broad desk, face freckled like a child's despite her chimney-smoke puff of white hair.

"What do you mean?"

"Listen to the difference. A Protestant asks, 'Why are there extra books in this Bible?' A Catholic asks, 'Why have these books been omitted from other Bibles?'"

"Well?" I prod.

"Well, what?"

"Isn't it the same answer either way?"

"Oh, no," she says, and a sly smile passes over her lips. "The way you phrase a question determines entirely the type of answer you'll get."

> FOR THE APPLE: *You are, by definition, round. You have a body people want to cuddle up to. You are not easy to dress, but have pillow-soft breasts and divinely sculpted ankles. For you, it's all about bringing focus to the top half, up and away from your tummy. Start by loving yourself enough to invest in a decent bra. Cap sleeves help to broaden your shoulders. Seek out tailored trousers that have no bulky pockets or protruding zips. Avoid clunky shoes—your body shape sits best atop a dainty wedge.*

The encyclopedia is a way to avoid phrasing questions, to skip directly to answers—or at least information. More and more I see how the attribution of meaning will come to rest with the reader. In this way, among others, I am becoming a Post-Modernist.

> A BRIEF HISTORY OF THE OLD TESTAMENT: *The Catholic, Protestant, and Orthodox churches all recognize the same twenty-seven books that make up the New Testament. There is disagreement, however, concerning the books that constitute the Old Testament. The Catholic Bible has seven books and parts of two others in the*

Old Testament that are not found in Protestant Bibles. Catholics describe these books as deuterocanonical, while Protestants describe them as apocryphal.

Deuterocanonical v. apocryphal, I sketch in my notebook. A Catholic answer and a Protestant answer. Both can be right, and both can be insufficient at the same time, I marvel. Without the seven chapters the Catholic Bible adds to "The Book of Esther," it bears the distinction of being the only book in the Protestant Bible that never mentions God—not even once. And one of the Catholic chapters in "The Book of Daniel" includes a dragon, which I think we all know opens the door to fairies and unicorns.

FOR THE SPOON: *Your woes lie around your saddlebags. But your top half is hard to fault. The name of the game is broadening your shoulders to balance those saddlebags. You are relatively flat-chested, so you can get away with higher-cut tops. A slashed neckline helps to give the impression of coat-hanger shoulders. Or use puffed sleeves to add vital inches! Your legs are short in comparison to the rest of your body. Wearing trouser hemlines to the floor is essential to maximize leg extension. A strapless dress is a wonderful thing for a Spoon. The stiff, flared skirt does an excellent job of disguising wide hips like yours.*

"Hello, Sister," I say, finding her on a stepstool dusting the shelves. She has cheesecloth in one hand, furniture polish in the other.

"Yes?"

"How are you today?"

"We both know that's not the question you want to ask." There is something both vexing and admirable about her ability to read my mind.

"What is the difference between *deuterocanonical* and *apocryphal?*"

She corrects my pronunciation and then replies: "Catholics believe the omitted texts from the Protestant Bible comprise a 'second canon'—that they are *deuterocanonical.* Protestants believe the texts added to the Catholic Bible contain valuable, historical information but are not divinely inspired; as a result, they cannot be considered part of the canon."

After a pause, what in poetry I will learn to call a *caesura*: "What do *you* believe, Sister Ann Cornelia?" It is a risky question, as I am sure nuns are expected to toe the party line.

She looks down at me, that sly smile again parting the plump flesh of her cheeks: "I tend to favor more information," she says, "not less."

"Even if it's controversial?" I press.

"If you think about it, really *think* about it, what information isn't?"

FOR THE RULER: *You might find it difficult to gain enough length in a sleeve or trouser leg, but being mostly tall, Rulers can carry clothes well. You have lovely long legs, lithe arms, and not too much flab around your girth—your only downfall is your need for shape. The most useful way to counter that is to break up your outline. A single-button jacket will always concentrate eyes on the center of your torso. A long A-line skirt pushes your waist upward, giving you a more womanly shape. Kitten heels add delicacy and curve to your otherwise straight figure.*

At the first mass of the new school year, Sister Mary Annette intercepts me on my way to communion. "It's OK," I whisper, "I've already been confirmed."

"Not in the Catholic tradition you haven't," she replies. I stare blankly into her face, the spider webs around her eyes. Her hand to my wrist, her body blocking mine: "Protestants don't believe in transubstantiation."

Now my lip quivers at the unfamiliar word. Now the other girls move past me, their ponytails swishing.

"The bread and wine carry different significance for Catholics," Sister explains, one hand pressing down on my shoulder now, holding me *sessile* as a plant—a word we have just learned in biology class. I'm not going anywhere.

Finally, I whimper: "What should I do?"

The other girls stand before the priest. He places the small moon of the wafer directly onto their tongues instead of placing it, Protestant-style, in the center of their open palms.

"There are two choices," Sister says. "You can cross your hands over your heart, and the priest will bestow a blessing. Or—if you prefer—you can simply kneel at your pew while the others go forth to receive the Eucharist."

"*Eucharist?*"

The other girls remain before the priest. He lifts a giant, silver goblet—a *chalice* I think it is called—and they sip from it, each after the one before her, as if they are not afraid of germs, as if they have never even heard of them. No one chooses her own small glass from the wheel of glasses, the round tray passed from penitent to penitent. The priest wipes the common cup with a white cloth, which is bound to stain. Later, I learn this is real wine, not grape juice, making them under-age drinkers, every one.

"*Eucharist,*" she repeats. "This is a sacrament in our faith. In yours, it is only a ritual."

Now the other girls step aside and pause (*caesurize?*) before the altar. They cross themselves before the twin statues of Jesus and Mary. But then I realize—*I* am the other girl here. They are not the others. They are the ones, the chosen ones, who know the words without even looking at their songbooks, who know as if by instinct when to stand, when to sit, and when to drop to their knees in synchronized supplication.

A BRIEF HISTORY OF THE EUCHARIST: *For Catholics, the sacrament of Holy Communion, or the Eucharist, involves transubstantiation, meaning the substance, or essence, of the bread and wine changes—in a real, fundamental, ontological way—into the substance of the Body and Blood of Jesus Christ. The word transubstantiation means that this change of substance is complete: The Body and Blood of Christ are not contained in the bread and wine, nor do they exist side by side with the bread and wine, as in consubstantial doctrines. The bread and wine are gone, completely replaced by the Body and Blood of Jesus. For Protestants, who most often adhere to the doctrine of consubstantiation, the bread and wine are symbolically, rather than literally, transformed by The Words of Institution.*

Transubstantiation v. consubstantiation, I sketch in my notebook. A Catholic story and a Protestant story. Could they both be right? Could they both be insufficient? I had taken communion since I was eleven, never considering there might be different interpretations of what we were doing at the altar. Confirmation was the affirmation of baptism. This meant that, since I couldn't remember being baptized as a baby, I had consented of my own preadolescent volition to become a dutiful disciple of Christ. The perks were wafers and grape juice during Sunday service and my own personalized offering envelopes, which came in the mail for all official members of the church.

FOR THE HOURGLASS: *Your body is the very essence of what makes a woman womanly! The key is to show it off. It is always difficult for an hourglass to look convincing in weekend clothes. Your shape is too ultra-feminine for trousers. Every item in your wardrobe should work clearly to define your curvy silhouette. Your waist is short and your crotch is long. The bluffer's way to longer legs is to find a top that is long enough to stop just below your crotch, fooling our eyes into not knowing where your legs end and your rump begins. Beware big loose bat wings or kimonos that will merge your chest and arms into one solid mass.*

At my grandmother's house, my father and his sister are playing Cribbage while my grandmother prepares a stew.

"I have a question for you," I announce, folding my hands on the table to convey the seriousness of the matter.

"Oh, no," my father jokes. "How much is this going to cost me?"

"It's nothing like that. It's about religion."

My grandmother, knowingly, over her shoulder: "What did I tell you would happen when you sent her to Catholic school? First come the questions, then come the doubts."

But I already had doubts! They had been with me long before Catholic school. If I was honest, they had been with me long before my first communion.

"Julie, don't believe a thing you hear at mass," Aunt Linda instructs. "All that pomp and circumstance violates the First Commandment."

"Well, I wanted to take communion at mass—"

"Oh, *God* no!" my father exclaims, his secret temper flaring. "That common cup alone is invitation to the Plague!"

"They wouldn't let me," I murmur.

"Good. We don't need them. We have our own communion on Sundays."

"But here's the *question,*" I say, feeling my frustration pooling in my palms. "When you take communion—each of you—what are you doing?"

"What do you mean what are we doing?" Aunt Linda leans in close to me, her green eyes scanning my face for further clarification.

"What do you believe it *means* when you eat the wafer and drink the juice?" I don't know how much more plainly I can state the question, and my feet tap impatiently on the floor as I wait.

"We believe we're receiving Christ's body and blood," my grandmother says. She wipes her hands on her apron and turns to face us at the table.

"*Literally,* or *metaphorically?*" I try to use my voice to italicize my words.

"Well, it's not *literal,*" my father says. "We're not *cannibals.*"

"See, Julie dear, it's a ritual." My grandmother pats my head. "We're remembering the sacrifice Jesus made for us on the cross."

"That's just what Sister Mary Annette said you'd say. She said Protestants believe it's a ritual, but Catholics believe it's a sacrament."

"It's a sacrament for us, too," Aunt Linda replies, her voice soft now, slow and deliberate. "Martin Luther named only two sacraments for Lutherans, as opposed to however many the Catholics have. Getting your car washed with holy water could be a sacrament as far as they're concerned." I frown to convey that this detour isn't useful to me.

"What are they?" I press. "The sacraments?"

"Baptism and communion. These are holy events in a person's life—and they *are* literal," she says.

My father sighs. "C'mon, Linda, what are you talking about? You're just going to confuse her."

"*I* believe that the bread and wine are altered when the minister blesses them. *I* believe the Holy Spirit comes into them and changes them so they are no longer ordinary bread and wine."

"You mean to tell me—" he leans forward now and pushes the Cribbage board away. "You mean to tell me that you believe we're eating the body and drinking the blood of Christ? That's ludicrous, Linda! The minister can bless it all till Kingdom Come, but put it under a microscope, and you'll see that nothing's different. Nothing's *altered.*"

"Linda," my grandmother murmurs, surprise and disappointment mixing in her tone, "where in the world did you get such a notion?"

"It's what I've always believed," she replies, rising to her feet and pushing in her chair. "Faith doesn't look through a microscope, Bill. Faith defies the laws of science. And now, if you'll excuse me . . ." She disappears into the hallway, and a moment later, we hear the door to her bedroom close.

"Well," I say, to no one in particular. "If Aunt Linda wanted to take communion at Catholic school, I don't think anyone would have any reason to stop her."

In World Cultures class, Ms. Curran prints the word **CATHOLIC** on the black chalkboard, then underlines it once for emphasis. "Who can tell me what this word means?" she inquires.

The room falls silent. A few girls turn to each other, arch eyebrows, shrug shoulders.

"OK. Let's try it this way. How many of you in this room identify as Catholic?"

All the girls except the tall one in the corner, the one with chlorine streaks in her curls and a bottom lip prone to quiver, raise their hands. "So—Erin, Emily, Somebody—tell me: what does Catholic mean to you? You must know what it means if you're going to claim it as part of your self-definition."

Ms. Curran is not a nun. Ms. Curran is a married woman who chose not to take her husband's name, who also chose not to have children. She represents to me a small fork along the monolithic path of possibility, that which is rarely mentioned when a girl receives her uniform and the first draft of her life's itinerary. Perhaps Ms. Curran too felt like an other, slicing her coffee cake in the faculty lounge between the long line of sisters, wedded to Jesus, and the short line of Mrs. So-and-Sos with their many babies and their battered mini-vans.

"Do you mean . . . like . . . *Roman* Catholic?" Emily clarifies.

"Well, that's a good point, Emily." Ms. Curran is invested in the snowflake view. To her, we are never just a cloud.

"Roman Catholic implies a certain set of convictions, of religious beliefs, doesn't it? But the word *catholic* all by itself, uncapitalized—it's an adjective. Does anybody know?"

I shake my head, but my notebook is open, my pen poised.

"It means universal, or inclusive, or all-embracing," she says, mingling among us, passing slowly up and down the aisles. "In some translations, it simply means whole."

"Is that because everybody's *supposed* to be Catholic?" Colleen asks, but when she glances in my direction, she blushes and turns away.

"You probably all know that the Roman Catholic Church was the first Christian church, so at one time, if you were Catholic, you were part of the whole of Christianity. This isn't true anymore. You can be Christian but not Catholic. The challenge for those of us who identify as Catholic is not to forget that spirit of inclusiveness, not to treat other Christians as—" she studies the red maple outside our window, searching for the right word—"*ersatz* Christians."

"What does that mean?" Erin wants to know.

"*Imitation,*" I say, clearing my throat. "Like a poor copy of an original."

That now was then. This now is later. I remember Ms. Curran with gratitude, her sincere desire to honor all traditions—she who taught the theology credit that no one else wanted to teach. World Cultures was code for all the others of the world, all the other ways of knowing, and coming to terms with the unknowable, that had been dismissed; that had been considered *ersatz,* less than.

How hard it is not to hold humanity to one standard, in all respects—religion, family, beauty. *Catholic* is a linguistic door that swings two ways: an impulse to include and an impulse to convert, depending on your interpretation of its meaning. The fraught imperative to accept yourself exactly as you are—*whole, complete*—and to do your best to conform to exactly what is expected of you—*universal.*

From "SLIM WAIST HOLDS SWAY IN HISTORY": *The common historical assumption in the social sciences has been that the standards of beauty are arbitrary, solely culturally determined and in the eye of the beholder. The finding that writers describe a small waist as beautiful suggests instead that this body part—a known marker of health and fertility—is a core feature of feminine beauty that transcends ethnic differences and cultures.*

Sophomore year we take Art Appreciation with Sister Janice. She is Catholic, as in Roman, but not lower-case catholic, not like everyone else. She even belongs to a different order. Sister Janice is what might be termed *sui generis,* a Latin expression meaning "of its own kind," unique in its characteristics. She is the only Dominican sister at Holy Names, the Snowflake's Snowflake, the Oddball Extraordinaire.

I like Sister Janice on principle: her rosy, age-defying face, her close-cropped, peppery- gray hair. She is a no-frills, no-gimmicks kind of woman, a fast talker, fast walker, ambidextrous artist and calligrapher. She also doesn't own any dresses, as far as I can tell, only white knee-high socks, colorful Capri pants, and Hawaiian shirts that billow at their too-big sleeves.

"The goal of this class isn't to teach you *what* to think about art," she says, skittering across the room like a stray marble. "It's to teach you *how* to think about art, questions you can ask, methods you can use."

Most of the students don't take Sister Janice seriously. They yawn and laugh, pass notes under the art room table. She is all whimsy on the surface, true, but I sense a sadness fuels her restlessness, a loneliness behind the neon flashes of her smile.

"How many of you have seen this painting before? Show of hands?" She projects a painting of three women standing naked together in a circle, their arms linked in partial embrace.

All around the room: small eruptions of nervous laughter.

"*None* of you? None of you have seen this painting—by Peter Paul Rubens, *the* Peter Paul Rubens?" Sister Janice uses italics in her speech just as I do. "*The* great Flemish Baroque master?"

Finally, a few girls concede, nodding: "Yes, we've seen it," Therese sighs, speaking on behalf of her friends.

"Observations? Remember: art history, art analysis, and art appreciation all come from the same place. They all start with seeing more clearly what is right before our eyes. *And*—" she whirls around—"being able to *articulate* what it is we see. Get it? *Art. Articulate.*"

I raise my hand and watch her face come to life like a candle flame. I start to say, "They aren't wearing any clothes"—which is the first thing *I* notice—but am superseded by Katie, who declares in a loud, exasperated voice: "They're *fat!*" Now her whole corner of the room rocks and roars with laughter. "What?" she snaps. "They are."

Sister Janice looks crestfallen, but she recovers by pacing to and fro in front of the open window, fingers laced behind her. "Well, *fat* is a pretty subjective term. What one person calls *fat* someone else might call *robust, hearty—winsome* even."

"They have big, dimpled butts," Therese says, emboldened by her friend's candor. "And rolls of flab."

"And cellulite," echoes a tinny voice in the back.

"Our task here is to try to understand what Rubens was doing, why he wanted to depict these subjects the way he did."

"I guess he just liked big butts, and he couldn't lie," a transfer student whispers behind me.

"It's quite easy," Sister Janice continues, "for us to confuse observation and interpretation. The brain, almost as soon as it registers an image, begins to interpret that image, and all interpretations contain judgments. We bring a lot of baggage to our interpretations, ideas about what our culture has taught us is beautiful."

When no one responds, Sister Janice projects a second image onto the screen. "This is a painting by Renoir. It was completed more than two centuries after the painting by Rubens. What do you notice?"

She is so hopeful, her body swaying from side to side, her eyes scanning the room for some sign of engagement: hands about to raise, lips about to part. "Anyone?"

I want to offer an insight. I want to make Sister Janice jump with joy and send her, like a wind-up toy, spinning around the classroom. But my tongue turns to sawdust in my mouth, and my ears burn red at the sight of so many bodies.

"The woman in this painting is less fat," Katie sighs. "Her skin is smooth by comparison—but she still has enormous thighs."

> From IBID: *Dr. Singh, from the University of Texas, has spent years examining representations of women throughout history* [. . .] *In his most recent research, he looked at how "attractive" women were depicted in literature, analysing more than 345,000 texts* [. . .] *There was a trend for slightly larger women in the 17th and 18th centuries—a trend typified by the paintings of Rubens—but demand for a slimmer waist was generally constant throughout the centuries.*

Thinking is long, and knowing is slow. This is what I have come to realize. Over the next two years, I return often to the distinction Sister Janice made between observation and interpretation. It was hard to have a pure thought. It was harder still to describe something without evaluating it. Looking at paintings in art class wasn't so different from flipping through *Marie Claire* or *Vogue* or *Vanity Fair.* Art and advertising were rife with women's bodies—all of them in varying states of undress. The viewer's eyes were reliably drawn to their cleavage, their midriffs, or their long, supple legs. Faces were rarely the focus, as portraits were less important than studies of physical form.

"Niki Taylor is *everywhere,*" Jasmine complains, back pressed against her locker, studying the newest issue of *Elle* like there will be a test tomorrow. "I swear."

"Don't you like her?" I ask.

"She's just so boring: blond hair, blue eyes, slender body, beauty mark . . . blah, blah, blah. We *get* it, you know. We've seen it all before. If you want to be *really* beautiful, try being a little different, a little less cliché."

This was the old snowflake theory anyway, but it seemed safer by all accounts to stay in the cloud.

"Tell me something," I say. "Doesn't it strike you as strange that girls spend so much time looking at pictures of other girls? I never see anyone with a men's magazine—not even men—but everyone stares at *Cosmo* in the checkout line."

"I'm not gay, if that's what you're getting at," Jasmine replies, sliding the magazine back in her bag.

"I didn't say that. I didn't mean that." *Why was everyone so defensive these days?* "I'm not even sure we're *meant* to look at all these women in a positive way."

Jasmine frowns at me. "Are you going to get all valedictorian about this and have to scrutinize it from every angle—because you *know* that gets on my nerves."

"I know. But—" she raised her eyebrows, as if to say *this better be good*—"just think about it: don't we mostly look at magazines to cut women down, to find the thing that's *wrong* with them? She's too this, or she's too that, or not enough of this, or enough of that—it's all I ever hear."

Jasmine takes out her Walkman, slides her earphones into her ears. This is her way of letting me know our conversation is over. "It's like a Where's Waldo game," I insist, "and we're always looking for the flaw."

Mrs. Korkowski is our math teacher. She is a tall woman shaped like a bell with beady black eyes, pallid cheeks, and a large, braided bun balanced atop her head like a knitting basket. Once a year, on Halloween, she lets her bun down, but the hair is so coarse and snarled and gray that everyone wishes she would pin it back up again.

Though she is a wife and mother, not a nun, Mrs. Korkowski is one of the few women I have ever met who seems entirely unconcerned with appearance. I suspect that even in the checkout line, she would be too consumed with quadratic equations or analytic geometry to even consider what newest bathing beauty graced the cover of which glossy magazine.

I like numbers, but I have a hard time with math. Unlike words, I don't relate to their practical applications.

"That's nonsense," Mrs. Korkowski says in our one-on-one review session. "You count every day, don't you? You measure things without even thinking. You follow recipes. You divvy up space in a drawer. *Math,*" she repeats.

"But that's *easy* math. I'm talking about the hard stuff."

"It's all hard to begin with," she replies in her cut-and-dry way. "But once you know it, you know it, and there's power in that."

"I do like the *language* of math," I tell her cautiously.

"For instance?"

"Well, this word *asymptote.* I like the sound of it."

"Me, too," Mrs. Korkowski says. "There's a poetry to math that most people miss entirely. Now tell me what the asymptote is."

"A line that is tangent to a curve at infinity," I repeat.

"Yes, yes, you're very good at memorizing, but what does that *mean?*"

Haltingly, I confess: "I think that's what I'm here to find out."

Now Mrs. Korkowski makes a snorting sound that is either a laugh or a sneeze. "Well, then. Let's try to get a handle on this, shall we? Let's interrogate the asymptote, figure out what purpose it serves. Any idea?" I want to say, *to make my life more difficult, unnecessarily,* but instead I hold my tongue and shake my head. "All right. Try this: asymptotes convey information about the behavior of curves. We use them to assess the nature of a curve."

This I understand. This I can grasp like a rock-climbing grip on the treacherous cliff of pre-calculus.

"So, break it down. What do we know about curves?"

That they're beautiful. That they're feminine. That you need them—but not too many or too much—for men to fall in love with you.

I flip through my notes. "That a curve can come close to a line without actually touching it?"

"Quite right—and you'll like this," Mrs. Korkowski says, with an almost-smile. "*Asymptote* is from the Greek for 'not falling together.' We assume that eventually the line and the curve will merge, but it's important to remember that in this context, the line and curve are idealized concepts." *Aren't they always?* "Their width is zero."

I write this down. "You know what other word I like? *Parabola.*"

"No tangents, please!" But then she laughs, in spite of herself.

> From IBID: *Dr. Piers Cornelissen, a psychologist at York University, says that the sexual attractiveness of the curve between slim waist and hips may be due to a liking for well-fed women rather than a subtle sign of fertility. His work uses mathematical equations to separate the amount of the "curve" between waist and hip* [. . .] *He said: "When we break apart that 'curviness,' it is almost impossible to find an effect for waist-hip ratio that is independent of effects such as body fat percentage."*

That now was then. This now is later. I have passed precalculus, as in *earned a grade above failing* and also *moved beyond it.* (Or so I thought.) In my grown life, I have become an asymptote of sorts, one who appraises the function of curves: curve balls in baseball, learning curves in classrooms. I live now in the era of Curves, the largest fitness franchise in the world, with machines designed especially for women.

A curve was once called a *curved line.* At some point in time, the curve and the line became separate, unique, making the curved line an oxymoron. Like *gay straight*—a contradiction in terms, an expression you never hear. I wonder about the place where a curve becomes a swerve: *to turn or be turned aside from a straight course*. I know what it means to swerve, suddenly, at the last possible moment—to avoid a collision (*two or more moving bodies exerting forces on each other for a relatively short time*). In other words, men and I have not fallen easily together. Tangentially, *Curve* is the nation's best-selling lesbian magazine.

INTERLUDE

From Robert Frost's AFTER APPLE-PICKING: *My long two-pointed ladder's sticking through a tree / Toward heaven still, / And there's a barrel that I didn't fill / Beside it, and there may be two or three / Apples that I didn't pick upon some bough. / But I am done with apple-picking now.*

We are not done, no matter what we tell ourselves. Not with diets, not with counting calories or measuring with spoons. Quotidian math: the math of preparation, proportion. Prufrock measured out his life with coffee spoons. We measure ours with artificial sweeteners: Splenda (as in *splendid*), Whey Low (as in *weigh low!*).

From Denise Duhamel's SPOON: *John Updike's image stays with me—his male character admires a slender / young woman whose collarbones strain toward each other and almost meet / in a dip where he envisions placing a teaspoon. I can't help but think / that this lovely girl could not let herself eat whatever was once in that spoon / on the spoon rest of her throat, whatever was cooking in her body that became / a willowy stove.*

I want to be the apple of your eye. But really, I want to be the spoon that rests between your collarbones.

(Watch out for those *dreaded saddlebags!*) But really, I want to be the equal in your life—or at the very least, the Equal in your coffee, your tea. I want to be the fruit of your fall, Eden worth forfeiting for me. I will spoon-feed you the best of my shiny red heart. I will be golden and delicious. But really, I want you to love my ass—or at the very least, to love my aspartame.

From Chris Abani's UNHOLY WOMEN: *But of course these poems are / about men, / which we become by defining how / we are not women / and / so becoming / a shadow devouring the light to find the limits.*

But really, I want to be your asymptote—to graph the function of $y=f(x)$—in which y=man and x=woman and f=faith that something will change. As things stand, a man equals a woman and then some. Plato says, *The measure of man is what he does with power.* What kind of ruler will he be? (She: *a Ruler who carries clothes well.*) But really, a ruler is a stick made of numbers and lines. If sticks and stones will break my bones, what will words do to me?

FROST: *For I have had too much / Of apple-picking: I am overtired / Of the great harvest I myself desired.*

DUHAMEL: *No matter how much I suck air into my throat, I can't / make a hollow place for a spoon on my neck.*

ABANI: *And of course there is God / and its problematic relationship to light / not to mention the question / of permission / who builds the box, the shape?*

Time has a shape. It is an hourglass. Beauty has a shape. It is an hourglass. (Or is it?) *Her skin is smooth by comparison, but she still has enormous thighs.*

⧗

Women had power in Catholic school. They were our teachers, our principal and deans, our former graduates who came back to brag about their good jobs on Alumnae Day. They comprised our student body. When we chose a leader, it was a given that the leader would be a girl.

Women were also our intercessors. In Lutheran church, you could only pray to God in his various forms, but in Catholic church, you could pray to all the saints, many of whom were women, and the most important of whom was Mary (*Holy Mary, Mother of God*). True, Mary did become a saint for reasons that seemed mostly beneficial to men and mostly beyond her control. For instance, I wasn't impressed that a twelve-year-old girl had managed to remain a virgin. God could have singled out any number of girls with compliant natures and unoccupied wombs to give birth to his son, but I did wonder why he chose to separate this snowflake in particular from that cloud.

On March 25 each year, we celebrated the Feast of the Annunciation, in honor of the day the Angel Gabriel appeared to the Virgin Mary and told her that she would conceive a child who would become the Savior of the world. This event was sometimes called "Lady Day," and every girl wore a floral dress and brought her favorite kind of flowers to place before the statue of Mary at the altar. Even Protestants were allowed to participate.

"You want to do what now?" my mother asks, studying her JCPenney catalog. Before I can answer, she holds up a picture of a woman in a long, low-waisted dress with frill sleeves and a sash trailing off to the side. "What do you think of this? Do you think I'm the right body type to pull this off?"

Aware of the thin ice beneath me, I tell her cautiously: "I think you should wear whatever you like, whatever feels comfortable."

My mother laughs wryly. "The two do not always go together." *Asymptote,* I muse—*beauty and comfort, a line and a curve.*

"It's the Feast of the Annunciation today," I say, clearing my throat, "so I need to bring flowers to school. I was hoping I could cut some lilacs from the side of the house. They're so beautiful, and they always smell so good."

"What's this Annunciation business all about?" she demands, suddenly suspicious.

"It's just a holy day at school. We have it every year. Remember?"

I follow her into the kitchen where she rummages through a drawer for her gardening shears—the small set with electric-orange handles. Unlocking the back door and stepping out into the sun, my mother squints as she begins to snip the fragrant lilacs from their boughs.

"You're not getting in too deep with this Catholic crowd, are you? I hope your father and I have made it clear that their entire religion is based on superstition and blasphemy, and their interpretation of the Scriptures is not to be trusted."

"I like mass," I say softly. In a weak and perhaps shallow moment, I confess it: "Mass is prettier than Lutheran church. The singing, the language, the look of things—it's almost *magical.*"

Now my mother holds the lilacs in her hands, not quick to surrender them to me. "Beware the seduction of beautiful things," she warns. *Who was she kidding?* "So often they are not what they seem."

"But what are they then?" I had felt excluded at mass before, restricted to my pew, resigned to my blessing, but I had never felt, even a little, deceived.

"What do you mean?"

"If things aren't what they seem, then what are they? What is it you think is going on?"

"Oh, come off it, Julie! All that hocus pocus with the priest and his ball of smelling salts. Not to mention—*praying* to women, *worshipping* Mary."

"It isn't worship exactly," I reply. "It's recognizing that we can learn from other people's experiences, that they might be able to help us along the way."

"They're *dead!*" my mother snaps, letting the screen door slam behind her. "They can't help you. Only Jesus can. The very idea . . ." Her voice trails off as she soaks a paper towel and begins to wrap it around the lilac stems, after which she will add a protective layer of foil.

Today I am feeling the opposite of Mary, not compliant at all—*defiant,* bold in my new opinions. "How is it any different," I argue, "this so-called *worshipping* of women we do in Catholic church—from the way we praise famous women every day?" My mother turns to look at me like I am a prophet bearing ominous news. "The secular culture worships women, too, and mostly for their bodies alone. Not even taking into account their virtues."

"How much more of this am I supposed to take?" Her cheeks crimson, her eyes filling with tears. "On top of everything else, are you going to tell me you're a *Catholic* now?"

"No. But I do say the 'Hail Mary,' not just the 'Our Father.' And I like the idea that women are thought of highly enough to be worth talking to. It isn't only about the men."

Now my mother—the most powerful person in our family—throws the lilacs into a cereal bowl and runs screeching through the house, calling for my father. "Bill! Your daughter has gone over to the dark side!"

In mass, my uncertainty resumes, grows back again like a weed or a flower—depending on your interpretation. Women couldn't be popes or bishops or priests; they couldn't pronounce the blessing over the bread and wine that may or may not become the actual flesh and blood of Christ. Tabloids reduced women to their bodies. It was true, I reasoned, not just an interpretation: *Julia Roberts stuns in gown with plunging neckline! Cameron Diaz looking svelte in designer bikini on romantic getaway! Madonna fans will be dazzled by her post-*

pregnancy weight loss glam! But when I thought about the women revered in Catholic church—really *thought* about them—weren't the most virtuous ones those who guarded their bodies like treasure? And then, if they didn't become nuns, the ones who surrendered their bodies to men and gave them children who bore their fathers' names? In Mary's case, she was a surrogate, a means for God to accomplish something he wanted, not truly an end in herself.

As my mother sometimes crassly said: "For men, having a child is ten minutes of fun; for a woman, a lifetime of pain and varicose veins."

Now the priest reads to us from *The Book of Luke*: "And in the sixth month the Angel Gabriel was sent from God unto a city of Galilee, named Nazareth, to a virgin espoused to a man whose name was Joseph, of the house of David; and the virgin's name was Mary. And the angel came unto her, and said, 'Hail, thou that art highly favored, the Lord is with thee: blessed art thou amongst women. And when she saw him, she was troubled at his saying . . .'"

I pictured her there, a dreamy girl, tall and sturdy with dark brown hair and a bottom lip prone to quiver; a smart seventh grader with no high school in sight, whose marriage to Joseph had already been arranged. *But what if she didn't want it, any of it?* What if she was a poet in her secret heart—the words falling from her tongue like the first soft flakes of winter snow—falling all the while as she scrubbed the floors, ironed the clothes, helped her mother prepare the meals? (*Holy Mary, the artist, the prodigy, or was she always destined to be—Holy Mary, little Ash Girl, little follower?*) What of those words she later scribbled on the Steno-pad beneath her bedside table, read back to herself late in the night while a lone candle continued to burn?

Now here's this angel, intruding on her solitude, cutting into the few quiet hours of her time between school and supper: "Fear not, Mary, for thou hath found favor with God.

And behold, thou shalt conceive in thy womb, and bring forth a son, and shalt call his name Jesus. He shall be called great, and shall be called the Son of the Highest . . ."

What if she had simply said *No thank you* and gone back to her chores? What if she had told the angel the name of another girl just down the road who had been saying how much she'd love to have a baby—someone who actually *aspired* to be a teen mom?

Instead, Mary acquiesced. She did as she was told. I thought of her leaning into that curve, turning, being turned, from her course.

Was canonization really worth it? Was intercession simply another chore? Think of the poems Mary could have written if she dared.

Now Sister Rosemary beckons to me, her broad shoulders straining against the snug of her blouse. "It's your turn, dear—to take your flowers to the altar."

I clasp the lilacs tighter in my palms, too dismayed at last to release them.

That now was then. This now is later. A quiet morning at college. A library book with an ominous name: *The Dead and the Living*. Inside I find a poem called "The Death of Marilyn Monroe." *When she died, did she shatter like an hourglass?* I wonder. *Did the sand of her scatter, then coalesce, mandala-like before the gusting wind?*

This poet is unfamiliar to me, a woman named Sharon Olds. I study her picture—the flowing hair, the knowing eyes—and muse how she is both at once: young in her face, old in her name. This, of course, is the paradox that Marilyn Monroe will inhabit forever.

As I read Olds's elegy, I reflexively bow my head. When I raise it again and gaze out the window toward the copse of blue spruce, the light curtain of fog, I find my thoughts have returned to Mary. It's not such a great stretch, though, is it—from *Mary* to *Marilyn?* The impulse is ibid; it comes from the same place. These women intersect: parabolas of heavenly light and not enough time. No asymptote in the world can save them.

> From "Secrets of Marilyn Monroe's Hourglass Figure Revealed in Receipts": *As the world's most famous sex goddess, Marilyn Monroe had to look after both her creamy complexion and her hourglass figure. Marilyn Monroe's diet has been revealed in a clutch of grocery store and meat market receipts. One substantial delivery was made two days before her big event of singing "Happy Birthday" to JFK. It's interesting to speculate why Monroe was buying so much food at this time, especially when she knew she had to be sewn into the gown she'd be wearing.*

> From "The Catholic Tradition": *Mary's body never knew sexual pleasure because her soul excluded it for the sake of God and mankind. She always exercised, as soon as her reason was able to understand, the virtue of chastity—that is, a rational and voluntary control over her entire psychosomatic human sexuality. Through her chastity and virginity, Mary consecrated to her Creator, in a total and absolute way, her human sexuality. She recognized the supreme dominion of God's absolute and eternal Being over her body, over the thoughts, desires, remembrances of her soul.*

Two women, embodied—whose bodies were not their own.

When I read "The Death of Marilyn Monroe" again several years later, I discover I have remembered it wrong. It begins with the men, the "ambulance men," whom Olds tells us are "never the same" after carrying the movie star's corpse from her home. (*Beautiful Marilyn, Mediatrix of All Grace! What was it they needed you to be for them—so they could go on living in the old way?*)

To see her dead, to feel her four limbs heavy and cold, her breasts "flattened by gravity," was to see her becoming human again. (*Your body is the very essence of what makes a woman womanly!*) They could hardly bear it.

Who would speak of a *mortal goddess* then—like a *curved line,* that contradiction in terms—that expression you never hear.

There is no scriptural record of Mary's last days on earth. Some traditions claim she went to Ephesus, where she met a peaceful, painless death (*dormition*). Others claim she remained in Jerusalem and was taken to Heaven without succumbing to death at all (*assumption*). In 1950, Pope Pius XII declared this latter belief official Catholic dogma. *Why?* Because they could not bear to see her dead, not even in dormition. Because they did not want to bear the "nightmares, strange / pains, impotence, depression" of what comes after such a death.

> $y=f(x)$—in which $y=$man and $x=$woman and $f=$faith that nothing will change

Bless them. Bless them to the four points of the compass, to the four corners of the room.

> In an unfinished letter to Joe DiMaggio: "*If I can only succeed in making you happy I will have succeeded in the biggest and most difficult thing there is—that is to make one person completely happy.*"

Bless them, I say. Bless them to their beautiful, four-chambered hearts.

> In response to the annunciation of the Angel Gabriel: "*Behold the handmaid of the Lord; be it unto me according to thy word.*"

But bless her, most of all, for she is all of us: "*just an ordinary woman breathing.*"

PART V

1. HAIR IS THE FIRST INHERITANCE.

Let H be the set of all natural numbers for which H ($n<1$) specifies women and H ($n>1$) specifies men. Hair is, after all, a gendered conundrum.

My mother tells the story of her French grandmother (H_1), still new to this country in her old age, quick to acquire its language, though resistant to its mores. (*Pluck this! Shave that! Disgraceful!*) Jacqueline (H_1) sits alone in her kitchen, across the alleyway from the house where my mother lives. They drink tea together in the afternoons, play cards, and peck at shortbread cookies. My mother has never felt so safe, so loved, as in the presence of this woman.

Let M be my mother's memory of Jacqueline (H_1), the way her eyes turn hawkish circles to those mesh-net stockings in the foreground of the frame. The sight of the legs there, short and spindly, crossed at the ankles in her plain taupe shoes, dominates this retrospective landscape: "The hair—it was effusive—black and thick and sprouting through the nylon squares. Even when I bought her an opaque pair, you could still see it, matted, dense." A dark tide rising beneath the surface.

Let Q be the question: "Why does it matter?"

Let T be my mother turning to me in the morning's half-light. "There are things a woman must do, if she discovers a deficit or an excess in her body."

"But I thought you didn't shave your legs on purpose. I thought you said it was unnatural."

Let U be my mother taking umbrage with my tone: "Does what I've described sound *natural* to you? The hairs on your legs are soft, golden. No one can see them. My legs are smooth without shaving. Why create a problem where none exists?" Then, extending her hand to me, I see my father's razor, the tin of Barbasol uncapped on the counter. "Your problem," she says, "is under your arms."

My father tells the story of his friend Roger (H_2), who was swarthy and dark with stubble that grew back by midday, a chest covered with a black carpet of hair. "Women always loved Roger," he explains. (*Let W be the wistful twinge of his tone.*) "He was fighting them off by fifteen. But the funny thing was, for all the hair he had on his body—" now my father laughs till his belly shakes, till the tears stream out of his eyes—"he didn't have two strands on his big, bald head."

Let Q be the question: "Why does it matter?"

My father stops suddenly. He is not prepared for a question like this and takes some time drying his eyes. "Well—I mean—the man is hairy as a gorilla, but his head is bare as a cue ball. And Roger was vain about his appearance, see—he never wanted anyone to know the truth, not even the woman he married. So he bought a toupee, wore it every day, and never told Janet about it. The first morning of their married life, she woke up, and there on the pillow beside her—" the shaky belly again, the teary eyes—"was the sum and total of Roger's hair! Can you imagine?"

Let I=I. I have thick, dark hair my mother calls *lustrous* and brushes with vigor. "We didn't get lucky with curls," she sighs, "but we did get lucky with texture. Someday," she assures me, "you'll meet the right man, and he will want you to let down your hair—to let it fall gracefully along your shoulders." (Given:

There is a direct relationship between quantity of hair and quality of desire.) "But this other business," she says, gesturing to the hollows of my arms. "Remember to keep it smooth there." I have thick, dark hair my mother calls *unsightly* and trains me to cut away. "The last thing you want is to give the impression that you're loose and ungroomed." (Given: *There is an inverse relationship between quantity of hair and quality of desire.*) "Men have no respect for a woman like that."

Let H_3 be my father, who was born with thick, blond hair, a cowlick resistant to trimming. "Both my children," his mother recalls, "were as golden as sheaves of wheat." (*Let P be the prideful twinge of her tone.*) At eighteen, the story goes, my father went with his father to the barbershop: a rite of passage. No longer would his mother dip her comb in water, snip his locks at the kitchen table. No longer would his sister sweep the stray gold away. "Short, but not a crew cut," my father says. The man mishears him. As the crew cut grows out, it is never golden again. He slicks back his thick, black hair with Brylcreem the way his father does: a rite of passage. He joins the ranks of men who are described as "tall, dark, and handsome." The new designation pleases him. Soon, his wife dips her comb in water, snips his locks at the kitchen table. As she sweeps the stray dark away, she notices the first strands of gray. It is almost overnight, this turning, this rite of passage. By forty, he joins the ranks of men who are described as "silver foxes." The new designation pleases him. If he is no longer young, at least he will be distinguished.

"Gray is good, but bald is bad," his wife tells him, running her fingers through his thick, gray hair. (*This is not her first binary.*) "Be glad you're the first. No husband of mine would be the second."

Let H_4 be the wife who is also my mother, who was born Snow White to her sister's Cinderella—the lesser princess of the darker hair. Their mother was famous for her favoritism, her preference for the fair. When my mother weeps over a storybook where Rapunzel's golden tresses form a ladder for her prince to climb, the older woman replies, "Not everyone can be beautiful." The younger woman invests in wigs, imagines a fairy godmother who transforms her into Twiggy. She marries a man who is tall, dark, and handsome. (*Men,* she notes, *need not be blond to be golden.*) When the daughter is born with thick, black hair, she remembers Snow White and mourns a little. The girl's hair lightens in the sun. There are hues of gold and red, touches of autumn. The daughter will not be overlooked. The daughter will not be forgotten after all.

Let H_5 be the daughter, who is also me. (Let $H_5 = I$.) Let the daughter find the mother's L'Oréal permanent color kits, the gloves laced with dye and balled in the trash, the empty bottles with the strong ammonia smell. The daughter knows better than to ask. She notes a small designation in the corner of the box: *gray-coverage guarantee.* When she is sixteen, the mother visits her in the turret of her loneliness. She comes bearing gifts: Dep styling gel and a crimping iron. "Men can go gray," the mother proclaims. "Women can't. Always remember that."

But the daughter doesn't understand. "Of course they can!"

"*No,* they *can't.*" The mother has declared her war on age and inheritance. "Your father gave you good teeth and great height, both of which will serve you well. But if you ever find your temples graying—if you ever notice strands of silver in your brush—promise me you will cover them up at once."

Let Q be the question: "Why does it matter?"

Her eyes narrowing, her jaw tightly hinged. We have come full circle in the morning's half-light, the last page of a script read over and over: "There are things a woman must do, if she discovers a deficit or an excess in her body."

2. THE BODY IS A TEMPLE.

Let B stand in for the body. Let B=T, for the body is a temple. Sometimes the body is a Shirley Temple (ST), a vessel of grace and good standing. But what of the body when it is not a Shirley Temple, when B ≠ ST?

The family is a constellation, recall. There are many simultaneous bodies in motion, which is another way of saying there are many temples in the sky. (*Ecumenism not given, not quite.*) This is why we pray toward Heaven. This is why we gaze toward the light. When we look up, we expect to see the parent planets. When they look down, they expect to see the child star.

Let 1984 be the Year of our Lord—Big Brother meets Only Child in the water-view, Republican suburbs. (*Recall that someone is always watching.*) Let TV be the small television set in our eat-in kitchen, where I study the girl (ST) in whose likeness I should have been formed. "She gave hope to millions," my father affirms. "She was the great cure-all for a nation's Depression."

Small and sweet, dancing and singing and smiling until her dimples are sore, I watch the little luminary revolve. This is the one who has come to eclipse me, my stationary body in the path of such extravagant light. Among her many names: *Bright Eyes, Curly Top, Little Miss Broadway, Rebecca of Sunnybrook Farm.* (*Let FE be my first fear of erasure.*) Later, add *Princess* and *Bobbysoxer.* Later still, beyond the script and screen, goodwill ambassador and soft cocktail: part ginger ale, part grenadine. (*A girl is sugar and spice and everything nice . . .*) But for now, for always, my mother cries: "Look at that bounty—all those perfect, natural curls!" (*Let HP be our middle-class cupboard, stocked with home permanent kits.*)

C_1 = First Correction: Shirley Temple's hair was actually thin and straight. Her mother rolled her curls by hand and pinned them in place—precisely fifty-six curls for each picture.

Dance lessons begin when I am five, the same age as Shirley Temple in her breakout film. (*Stand Up and Cheer!*) She is like a comet I am chasing through the galaxy, bright enough to trace with the naked eye. Before the bathroom mirror, I learn to worry over my body, to wonder who would ever worship at this temple of pink tights and striped leotard. I recite it like a pledge: *the first commandment of girlhood is to be adored.* And the corollary ($g+1$): *the second commandment of girlhood is to be adorned.*

"Light on your feet!" Miss Erika insists. "Imagine you are gliding through the clouds!"

What to make of my long, inflexible legs moving crudely through the atmosphere? (*My stringy arms? My doughy center?*) What to make of this body for which I am certain no one will ever stand up and cheer?

D_1 = First Discrepancy: Shirley Temple's mother was paid $150 a week as her daughter's coach and hairdresser—this during the Great Depression. My mother receives no compensation for her travail—this during the Reagan Revolution. (*A deficit and then an excess in the national body . . .*) I marvel that Shirley Temple (ST) and Ronald Reagan (R^2) were both movie stars, adept at receiving and radiating light.

Let ME be my mother in that era, standing before the bathroom mirror, brandishing her curling iron like the barrel of a gun. *This is a stick-up,* she might have said, as I perched on the toilet seat, the pink tulle of my tutu wilting beneath my sweaty palms. When I stand for her, twirl and curtsy and imagine the auditorium crackling with applause, it does not escape me—the purse of her lip, the crease in her brow.

Let HQ be the hard question that sticks to the roof of my mouth. "Is there—something *wrong* with my body?"

"Don't say *body,*" my mother instructs. "For girls, we say *figure.*"

"And for boys?"

"*Physique.*"

Let F be the figure and G be the ground. (In another version of this story, G is the girl and S is the stage.) There is no relationship between them that is not fraught. There is no relationship between them that is not complicated by perception. (Given: *To be is to be perceived.*) Shirley Temple cradles a Juvenile Oscar at the 1934 Academy Awards. (*I play a boy in a 1986 production of the Nutcracker ballet.*) Shirley Temple presses her tiny hands and feet into wet cement at Grauman's Chinese Theatre. The moviemakers praise her, promise she will be immortalized. (*I fall and sprain my wrist roller-skating. Brandon, Punky Brewster's dog, is hit by a car. Mr. Keaton has a heart attack on* Family Ties. *I realize with a growing terror that anyone can die at any time.*)

The body may be a temple, but it fails as an oracle. (*Nobody, it seems, can predict the future.*) Shirley Temple debuts in Technicolor as *A Little Princess,* her final box-office success at the age of eleven. I dress as a princess for my final Halloween. My mother chides me for wearing too much makeup. (*There's a line you mustn't cross between looking good and Lady of the Evening!*) Here conflicting accounts occur. Eager to make the transition from child star to teenaged actress, Temple turns down MGM's offer to play Dorothy in *The Wizard of Oz.* Instead, she assumes the role of *Susannah of the Mounties* for Twentieth Century Fox, a performance panned as lackluster by her critics and fans. In another version of this story, MGM casts Temple as Dorothy in *The Wizard of Oz,* but she is soon replaced by Garland when they realize she can't carry the film's more sophisticated tunes, can't make the transition from girl to grown-up ($G_1 \rightarrow G_2$).

Shirley Temple retires from show business at the age of twenty-two. Judy Garland takes an overdose of barbiturates at the age of forty-seven. Nobody can predict the future. (*Or can she?*) Nobody is immortal. (*Or is she?*) One woman endures, one woman expires, but both women live on. (*Legacy. Posterity. Their hands and feet in wet cement at Grauman's*

Chinese Theatre.) But which is the figure, you ask, and which the ground?

Let G = Gestalt: *an organized whole that is perceived as more than the sum of its parts.*

Figure-ground illustrations are an important tool of Gestalt psychology. The most famous figure-ground illustration is the Rubin vase, developed by Danish psychologist Edgar Rubin circa 1915. (*Note: Edgar Rubin ≠ Peter Paul Rubens, the Flemish painter who rendered women's curves on canvas.*) Rubin specialized in ambiguous pictures. There is a vase in the center and a face matching its contour on either side. (Given: *The body is a vase, a vessel; the body has a face, a profile.*) Two shape interpretations are possible, but only one can be maintained at any given moment in time. (*To <u>have</u> a body? To <u>be</u> a body?*)

All figure-ground illustrations demonstrate at least one of these patterns:

a. The figure and the ground compete. (*Sometimes the vase is the figure, the face is the ground.*)
b. The figure should be the ground and the ground should be the figure. (*Sometimes the face is the figure, the vase is the ground.*)
c. The figure and the ground create an optical illusion. (*Always, the girl is an optical illusion.*)

Who would you rather be—Shirley Temple or Judy Garland? (*These are the templates of girlhood available to us at this time.*) Both diminutive entertainers, both emblems of innocence and grace. *Good girls,* we might call them. One named after a sacred place; the other after a wreath of flowers, a decoration.

"I'd love to see you on the cover of the Penney's catalog," my mother wishes aloud. "My sister would open her mailbox, and—"

"And what?"

"Well, let's just say it's a sight that would shut her up for good."

I am the figure, but I feel more like the ground.

My mother takes me to church and Sunday school. She places fresh-cut flowers on my bedroom windowsill. "When you grow up, you can compete for Miss America. When you win, they'll give you a crown and a sash and a big bouquet of roses."

I have a figure, indistinguishable from the ground.

But truthfully—who would you rather be? I ask this question to no one in particular. (My diary perhaps.) The answer depends on whether you'd rather be remembered for "The Good Ship Lollipop" or "Over the Rainbow." (It does not escape me that both songs are fantasies of escape.)

In the outer solar system, comets are nearly impossible to detect due to their infinitesimal size. (*My presence was always easy to detect. I never flew under anybody's radar.*) As a comet approaches the inner solar system, the sun's radiation causes volatile materials within the comet to vaporize and stream out of the nucleus. (*However, it should be noted: I was never good at letting off steam.*) A huge, extremely tenuous field hovers around the comet, and from this field a tail is formed. (*Knowing little about astronomy, I am likely to confuse a comet with a star, particularly a comet with a falling star.*) In astrophysics, there is a concept called a "tail disconnection event." (*I believe the synonym in psychology is "adolescence."*)

Let A = Adolescence: *a disorganized hole that is perceived as a bottomless pit.*

Watch how the formulas become more complicated now. Notice the deficit of real numbers, the excess of fractions. Anticipate equations that do not balance nicely on both sides.

I ≠ ST. I ≠ JG. Δ *I am a figment of someone's ungrounded imagination.*

3. AGE BEFORE BEAUTY.

Let T = theorem. Let T = a general proposition not self-evident but proven by a chain of reasoning; a truth established by means of accepted truths.

Let I = idiom. Let I = a group of words established by usage as having meaning not deducible from those of the individual words. (Let I = G, as in *an organized whole that is perceived as more than the sum of its parts.*)

Let group of words = *general proposition* and usage = *accepted truths*. Therefore, let T = I.

If we accept the truth of certain idioms, we begin to literalize our metaphors. For instance, what does it mean to "tap-dance like mad" or to "do a tap dance for someone"? Patterns of usage suggest the phrase implies *to have to move fast and/or talk cleverly in order to distract and/or appease someone.* (A parent perhaps? The culture at large?) Being no prima ballerina and not confused on this point, I transpose myself easily from key to key. My mother enrolls me in a tap-dancing class. (Let $V_{ivacity}$ replace G_{race} in the new equation.) What I remember: Miss Melanie was pregnant most of the time. Her tap shoes had grown-up heels. At home, I practiced with my mother in the basement on a wooden board. (*Shuffle ball change. Shuffle ball change.*) She knew how to tap-dance from her high school days. (Let $L_{iteral} = M_{etaphorical}$ here.) Soon, she said, I would be ready to tap-dance like mad for anyone I ever met.

"The longer you live, the more you lose," my mother had been known to say. (*Transposed*: "Age before beauty.") When he held the door for me, my father had been known to say, smiling, "Beauty before age, my dear." For a while, you are too young for everything, always "too young to understand." But then, innocence gives way to new imperatives. The Poet writes: *to turn woman is to turn / body.* As in the more advanced math, arrows become bi-directional (↔), meaning the equation is reversible. (*Transposed*: "Nothing is permanent.") (*Transposed again*: The possibility of a second chance.)

I watch my mother ready herself in the morning. She does her leg lifts to keep her thighs tight and toned, then presses her arms against the doorframe until her chest juts out in her Playtex Cross Your Heart bra. "Isometric exercise," she replies without being asked. "I don't want my triceps flapping around like a flag." Then comes the perfume, daubed behind her ears and rubbed between her wrists—oily and sweet like flowers in a frying pan. Deodorant (non-negotiable) under her arms. Between her waist and legs, the place without a name (N_0), she powders heavily so the hair turns white as George Washington's head. That's when she catches me smirking. "What is it?" she says. "You think good hygiene is *funny?* You think it's *funny* to want to smell good?" I climb the wall with my eyes, up and away. "Just you wait," my mother warns. "You think it's all a free ride now, but one day you'll have to pay the toll."

Instead, I picture the Troll under the bridge—in Fremont, where we went once on a field trip. Our teacher read us a story about three goats who wanted to get across, about the Troll who stops them and threatens to gobble them up. Then, the image comes alive like a movie reel. It is raining. I am wearing my purple galoshes, which are far too small for me now. For some reason, I have set out to cross this bridge alone.

"What are you?" the Troll wants to know.

"A girl," I tell him.

"Not likely. What are you really?" he asks, sniffing my clothes.

"I really am a girl."

"Maybe you *were* a girl at one time," the Troll replies. "But you're something different now."

"What?"

I rejoin my mother's soliloquy in progress: ". . . and no boys are going to want to have anything to do with you if you don't keep your body-scents under control."

"I don't know," the Troll says, "but—*you stink.*"

Later, in bed, I conjure the Troll again. I conjure the sign he has hung on the bridge, those arrows pointing in two directions (↔). "What now?" he demands, trudging up the stairs, appraising me with arms akimbo. I notice his beard is gnarled and his breath is bad. His chest is heaving from the hard climb.

"Why don't you stay in the toll booth?" I ask, pointing over my shoulder.

"Why don't you mind your own beeswax?"

"OK," I say. "Well . . ."

"Well, what? I haven't got all day."

"I'd like to cross over again."

"Sorry, Sugar Plum. It doesn't work that way."

"What do you mean?"

"I let you through once. No big deal. You were reeking like an oyster tin left out in the sun." He clamps his nose and waves his hand for effect.

"But the road goes both ways."

"Who says?"

I gesture toward the sign.

"Don't confuse *or* with *and,*" he warns. "Common mistake, but it'll get you into trouble every time."

"So this is an *Or* bridge, not an *And?*"

"That's right, Witch Hazel. Coming *or* going. One *or* the other. You can't have it both ways."

"But if I can't go back the way I came, where should I go from here?"

"*Forward!*" cackles the Troll. "Now be gone with you, Jujube." I am halfway across the bridge when I hear him call after me: "If you want something reversible, try your raincoat!"

I am still thinking about the significance of the reversible raincoat when I realize someone is staring at me. This is the end of elementary school, the last summer of Vacation Bible School, the great fork in the road. (*I picture it, too—that gleaming fork—its shiny, silver tines.*) Chavonne is one of the pretty girls, whose likeness can be found on the cover of books like *Sweet Valley High*. Whenever possible, I try to avoid her eyes.

"Hey, hey," she whispers. "It's Judy, right?" There is no point correcting her, and so I nod. "Do you want to trade me those pixie sticks for these jolly ranchers?" (*Let R be my resignation—giving whatever is asked, taking whatever is offered.)* I watch as she glosses her lips, then smooths her hair into a low, silky ponytail.

"Judy, you know what?" I shake my head. Chavonne chews Doublemint gum, even though gum-chewing isn't allowed. She wears a body spray her sister bought at Victoria's Secret. Her T-shirts are all from the Gap, and her jeans are all from Banana Republic, and her sneakers have little blue squares marked KEDS on the heels—to distinguish them from imposters. (*How is it that I know all these things about her, and she doesn't even know my name?*) "I found out they're going to make us dance."

"What?"

"Genevieve just told me. The teachers are going to make us do a *tap dance* for them."

"But we don't have any costumes, any tap shoes! Are they even going to give us time to choreograph a routine?"

That's when I realize Chavonne is laughing at me, that Genevieve is laughing at me, too, from across the room—that they are both being skinny and blond and pretty and laughing at me with their high, tinkly voices. "*Oh. My. God.* You fell for it. You *totally* fell for it!"

"I did not! I knew you were kidding the whole time. *I* was the one pulling *your* leg."

Chavonne's glossy lower lip gapes in horror. "Gross!"

"It's an *expression!* It's just an expression." (*Let D be my desperation, begging to be believed.)*

I watch the friends exchange glances, mouth silent words. Then, Chavonne rolls her legs under her body, sits up high on her heels. "Here's an expression for you," she murmurs. "Keep your hands to yourself."

Let L = Lamarck, Jean-Baptiste (1744–1829). Let MS = middle school, where I first encounter his name. Let IAQ = inheritance of acquired characteristics, the concept attributed to Lamarck, sometimes known as "soft inheritance." Let L + MS + IAQ = another way of regarding the world.

In theory, an organism can pass on traits acquired during its lifetime to its offspring. Think of the giraffe with its long neck, the blacksmith with his muscular arms. And if my mother were angry, say, her anger might grow more firmly in me. And if my father were passive, say, his passivity might root more deeply in me. (Let $A_{nger} + P_{assivity}$ complicate the old equation.)

But then a new term arises, phoenix from the ash of the Given, the non-negotiable: *Xenogenesis* (X). Let X = production of offspring entirely different from either parent. Could I = X? (*A penny in a wishing well at the over-air-conditioned mall.*) The gestalt again, transposed: that I could be more and other than the mere sum of their parts.

"I have to ask you something," I say, materializing in my grandmother's kitchen.

"Oh, you startled me, dear. I didn't even hear the door."

"It's about Great Aunt Ethel." Her lips close softly; her smile recedes. "May I look at her picture again?"

She nods and gestures toward the cupboard where the memory boxes are stored. Aunt Linda, who has come for dinner and to wash her clothes, appears on the landing with laundry basket in hand.

We settle together at the kitchen table, the two grown women with coffee in their cups, their faces and habits that resemble each other. "Grandma, you said once you'd tell me her story—your sister—the one who died young." I slide the picture of Ethel toward her. She is golden, luminous, at once a rising and a falling star.

"What is it you want to know?"

A bright meteor of a word—small body of matter, soft streak of light: "*How?*"

There is a long, cosmic sort of pause before she answers: "Ethel starved to death." My eyes turn to question marks. "Which is to say—Ethel starved herself to death."

"Suicide?" I gasp.

"In a way. She was so young and so beautiful, but she couldn't see herself that way. Ethel always wanted to be smaller, more of the arrow shape that was popular in those days. So she started taking diet pills, and she stopped eating anything real. Her husband, Oscar—he was beside himself. He wrote to us from New York, where they were at the end, told us she'd been hospitalized. But you can't force someone—you can't." My grandmother's voice is shrinking in her throat. "In the end, it was all too much for her heart."

"Do you remember her?"

She nods. "She was ten years older, but she was—well, she was unforgettable, always dancing and singing and putting on little shows. Wait. I think I still have—" As she sifts through the box, Aunt Linda catches my eye.

"Are you doing a project for school? Some kind of family tree?"

"Sort of," I say.

"Here it is. This isn't a professional picture, but it's from before—before Broadway and all that business." My grandmother hands me a faded snapshot of a teenaged girl leaning against a rock wall, grinning from ear to ear. "She was probably sixteen there, maybe seventeen. We lived in Canada. That was taken just down the road from our home. Oscar may have taken it. They were sweethearts even then."

We all peer at the picture together, this relic from our collective past. "I see a little of Linda in her there," my grandmother says. "A little of you, too, dear. She had a contagious kind of joy. People sought her out. They liked to be around her."

I recognize something in her posture, the way she uses her hands in her pockets to pull the coat closer around her. The desire to be covered, to be contained. Suddenly: "Is that a raincoat she's wearing?"

"Ah yes, her beloved Macintosh. In the spring, she never wore anything else."

"Was it reversible?" (*Let WA be the wild anticipation in my tone.*)

"No," my grandmother smiles, shaking her head. "They didn't have those until much, much later."

4. ALL BLOOD IS BAD BLOOD.

Let B = the set {Blood, Beauty, et al.} Let S = the set {Science, Story, et al.} Let all the letters be multivalent, just as they always are.

Let C = the set {Change, Constant, et al.} Let T = the set {Transmutation, Truth, et al.} If change is the only constant, then transmutation is the only truth. In simplest terms, transmutation means *the action of changing or the state of being changed into another form.* Like all changes, it may be passive or active, chosen or random. Like all changes, its reversibility remains unclear: → *and/or* ← *and/or* ↔. The use of *and/or*, as with *?!*, as with ±, is often an anxiety-ridden designation.

Pearl Buck once wrote, "There is an alchemy in sorrow; it can be transmuted into wisdom." What she failed to specify is how.

Let A = the set {Alchemy, Allegory, Analogy, Adolescence, et al.} Note how the simple act of parataxis—placing terms or objects side by side—seems to imply a relationship among them. This may (or may not) result in faulty logic.

What we understand is that alchemy is a form of transmutation. It is widely regarded as a proto-science, a template upon which subsequent science was built. A medieval forerunner to chemistry, one premise of alchemy is the transformation of baser metals into gold. (Alt. *The story of Rumpelstiltskin, in which a captive young woman is commanded to spin straw into gold.*) A broader premise of the term is that it signifies a process by which paradoxical results are achieved or incompatible elements combined with no obvious rational explanation. While alchemical processes would seem to contradict theorems proven by a chain of reasoning, such processes might be accurately described as resulting in gestalts: *configurations or patterns of elements so unified that their properties cannot be derived from a simple summation of their parts.*

Let Q be the question: "Why does it matter?"

Because there is something alchemical about the girl (G_1), about the gestalt (G_2) she is expected to form. (*What is the difference between a gestalt and a mosaic, between a gestalt and a collage? Does it have to do with how readily each can be parsed, how apparent its separate elements are?*) There is something inexplicable about her transmutation from G_{irl} to W_{oman}, $G_1 \rightarrow W_1$. (*What is the difference between transmutation and metamorphosis? Does it have to do with becoming something else altogether versus becoming a new version of the same old story?*) I want to understand this ($G_1 \rightarrow W_1$), which will require a reversal of sorts ($W_1 \rightarrow G_1$ *and/or* $G_1 \leftarrow W_1$), a reopening of certain case files.

The Menses (M_1) is a Case in Point.

April 1992. I wake in a twin bed beside my grandmother. The bed once belonged to her husband, who died eight years before I was born. I am twelve now, I am torn, I am in love with old words and *cast asunder* even from myself. I once saw lightning split a tree trunk in a movie and thought, *There, that is my story.*

In the night, I have crossed over the bridge of no returning. (*Menarche.*) In forty years, another bridge will come into sight. (*Menopause.*) I am a tongue-tied Eve in a post-lapsarian garden, and all these new words are lost on me. On the way to the bathroom, a transmutation will occur: a new era of passive voice, of third person.

$G_1 + M_1 = \Delta$

Which is to say: Blood alters the Girl. She is newly aware of the set she contains. (The churchwomen's advice: *Think of the eggs you're carrying, the future lives. From now on, you must carry your body as you would carry a basket full of breakable things.*) Which is also to say: A macroscopic change has occurred in the value of the variable.

Let A = the set {Alchemy, Allegory, Analogy, Adolescence, et al.} Let A = Allegory, in particular.

The Girl (G_1) feels a renewed kinship with the old fairy tales, the ones her father once read to her before bed. She has knives in her belly now, a sign of the curse her mother always warned her was coming. She drinks tea sweetened with honey, pretends it's a potion to lessen her pain.

Now she notices how all the girls ($G_{\text{et al.}}$) in fairy tales are lost. Are they *wayward* also? Is this what is meant by *a home for wayward girls*?

All the girls ($G_{\text{et al.}}$) in fairy tales are required to descend. Later, she will learn a word for this, too: more precise than *down,* more concrete than *changed.* The girls in fairy tales are fated for *katabasis.*

Think of Little Red Riding Hood, the Everygirl (EG) in her cloak of new blood. Hadn't she walked to Grandmother's house any number of times? But it was not until now, where this new story begins, that the Wolf grew inclined to pursue her. The Girl (G_1) sits propped in her proper bed. The wicker structure behind her head transmutes to a trellis where early roses struggle to climb. It is as the Poet says: *I was a girl then, my chest its own walled garden.*

Riding Hood leaves her parents' house with picnic basket in hand. She has been warned, as she always was, that she must adhere to the path. Perhaps she is walking more slowly this time? Perhaps she grows distracted by a new scent in the air, a shift in the seasons? It is April no doubt, so the hood shields her head from a soft, spring rain. Even the sticker bushes are beginning to bloom.

And mustn't she proceed *over the river, and through the woods*? Isn't that always the way to Grandmother's house we go? All those other times, when she reached the landform at the mouth of the river, the water was low, and the Everygirl (EG) stepped easily across. Now, at the Delta (Δ), she sees the tide is high from heavy rain, and the current is strong from the tug of the moon. And hadn't a teacher once told them all, with a faraway look in her eyes: *Your cycles are controlled by the moon. Young ladies have a special relationship with the lunar world.*

The Girl (G_1) sits propped in her proper bed. Moonlight streams through the pink lace curtains. Outside: a suburban street on the edge of the known world. Wasn't it true that wolves, too, had a special relationship with the moon?

"I can help you across if you like," he offers. The Everygirl (EG) is well-trained in dread. She knows this Wolf (W) who appears beside her stands for everything she was meant to fear. He is the archetypal Stranger, leering from his car, handing out candy on the public library stairs. But like the Troll under the bridge, she senses his presence is necessary for her passing.

"We must get on with it after all," the Wolf smiles, and his teeth glint yellow as sulfur in the strange, alchemical light.

"With what?" she asks. The cool sediment and river-water seep slowly into her shoes.

"Why, with your katabasis, of course!"

Let A = the set {Alchemy, Allegory, Analogy, Adolescence, et al.} Let A = Adolescence in particular. The Wolf (W) is suddenly younger. The Girl ($G_{\text{et al.}}$) notices bare patches in the new growth on his chest, skin beneath it that is pink as berries, soft as silt. She senses the loneliness beneath his bravado, the sadness in his bays at the moon.

"It isn't your grandmother I came for, you know."

She nods, climbing onto his back. "I am familiar with this story. I know you will want something in return."

They ford the river together, her face pressed into his fur. There is a faint, metallic scent about his neckline, which she will learn is the way blood smells as it dries.

In the woods, the Girl observes that all the trees have severed trunks, split at the root by lightning. She suddenly understands that she is not special, e.g., $G_{irl} = E_{very}G_{irl}$.

"I want what's in your basket," the Wolf says. It is unoriginal, and he blushes as he tells her. "I'm sorry. We hunt. That's what we do."

"Should I run away then?"

"If you wish." His eyes are hazel. They switch between green and brown, glowing. "Of course I will catch you, but I always enjoy the thrill of the chase."

"I could surrender," she posits.

"If you wish." His voice is still high like the boys she knows, the ones who clear their throats and widen their stance and spit into the playground dust.

"OK then."

"OK then."

But she doesn't run, and she doesn't put down the basket. She is filled with some other power. Somehow—she is not even sure of it herself—the Girl scales one of the trees with the severed trunks. It is katabasis in retrograde: an ascent, a palinode.

The Wolf (W), who is also a boy in men's clothing—heavy flannel and steel-toed boots—gazes up at her and begins to howl. "How can you do this to me? It isn't the way," he pleads. "It isn't the way it's supposed to be."

She shrugs her shoulders. She is a great martial in the art of waiting.

"If you stay there too long, everything will spoil. Overripe fruit always falls to the ground."

She shrugs her shoulders again and stretches her legs the length of the bough. He will not faze her.

Now the Wolf (W), who is also a story she will not soon forget, flashes his teeth, his broad mouth foaming. "You'll rot," he says. "You'll shrivel up, and fall to the ground, and die."

She shrugs her shoulders. "Maybe. But I think I'll just watch for a while."

$G_1 + M_1 = \Delta$

In the distance, she could see a Girl (G_1) cresting the hill, beginning her slow descent into a concrete valley. The sidewalk came in predictable squares, but a lush green moss grew in the crevices. The Girl was not beautiful, or ugly, or ordinary, or exceptional. She was almost all of these, and not quite any of them—which is how it is to be a girl at the center of a looming equation.

The Girl has just left her grandmother's house where, earlier that morning, she discovered blood seeping from a wound she had not known was there. Perhaps she fought a battle in her sleep? Perhaps it was a dream-wound and would close soon on its own? The girl was remarkably naïve about her own body. But she was singing, and it was her song that the Everygirl (EG) in the tree recalled and thought of for many moons after:

A-tisket a-tasket
A green and yellow basket
I wrote a letter to my love
And on the way I dropped it,
I dropped it,
I dropped it,
And on the way I dropped it.
A little boy he picked it up and put it in his pocket.

5. ALL DATING IS CARBON DATING.

Let Date (D_1) = the day of the month or year as specified by a given number. Let Date (D_2) = a sweet, dark brown, oval fruit containing a hard stone. Let Date (D_3) = a romantic rendezvous arranged in advance at an appointed place and time.

Let all the letters (D_{1-3}) be multivalent, just as they always are.

I am back in my own skin again, reflexive as ever. (I = I). I have seen productions of *Prelude to a Kiss, Barefoot in the Park,* and most recently, *The Phantom of the Opera.* In ninth grade, we read *Romeo and Juliet,* a love story that features youths as hapless and foolish as ourselves. We hate them for being everything we are, and for reminding us.

Then, we watch the movie. Juliet, as portrayed by Olivia Hussey, is indisputably beautiful. I am reminded in particular of the large gulf—oceanic really—between a *Julie* and a *Juliet.* I hold new reverence for the *t* that confers such beauty. (If $T_{ruth} = B_{eauty}$, then $B_{eauty} = T_{ruth}$.) I must be something else then, something other.

Consider the evidence: Juliet has many suitors; I have none. Juliet dies young and desired; I fear I will die old and alone. Yet Juliet is also a poet, a designation I claim for myself—*when he shall die, take him and cut him out in little stars, and he will make the face of heaven so fine.* Love must be the ultimate transmutation, I marvel, that a girl with this shiny black hair, this smooth, blemish-free skin, finds such words to describe a boy who is, as far as I can tell, simple and plain. Love must open in us a new set of eyes.

The teacher notes on my essay, "Good effort. Don't forget to work from the text, not just the film. Olivia Hussey portrays one version of Juliet, but Shakespeare's character is immortal!" (And dead at thirteen?) But I could see through the lattice of the word *immortal—that which never dies*—to the wild garden that grew behind it. Juliet lived on like Marilyn Monroe or Princess Grace or the Holy Virgin whose image faithfully adorned our halls. She lived on as the transfigured female body, too beautiful to forget.

Juliet was different, though. Juliet had felt and professed her own desire as well. The other women—they were worshipped, they were praised—but had they swooned the way Juliet describes in her breathy soliloquy, the white tunic slipping low on her white shoulder like the curve of the moon?

O, I have bought the mansion of a love, but not possess'd it!

"She wants to date him," I murmur.

"No," the girl beside me says, Rapunzel-like, her long trellis of curls. "She wants to *fuck* him."

In one room, we study the tragic love stories of British literature, all the Romantic poets; in another, just across the hall, radiometric carbon dating.

"Welcome to Chemistry," Mr. Nowak proclaims. He is the only man-teacher in our all-girls school—but is he lonely, a foreigner washed up on this female shore? Or perhaps he likes it, lone Wolf among so many rosy Riding Hoods.

"If your hair were ever to catch fire," he says—"a great many of you have long, lustrous hair"—I watch as he scans the room, his eyes never alighting on mine—"this is where you should go." There is a little shower at the back of the class, a black curtain that you can draw closed. From a distance, it looks like a magician's box, the kind the assistant steps inside and from which she disappears.

"Chemistry," Mr. Nowak says, "is the science of matter." (Let Q be my persistent question: *Why does it matter?*) "We are interested here in atoms and their interactions with other atoms—how they react, the kinds of bonds they form. Chemistry is the relationship science."

The golden hairs on my arms prickle and rise. I long to understand the science that underwrites such lines: *Hood my unmanned blood bating in my cheeks, With thy black mantle, till strange love, grow bold!*

When I think about the girls in fairy tales, as I often do, I realize they never date the men they marry. We never see the gardenia corsage, the red rose boutonnière, the young sweethearts posing at the hearth while someone's parent snaps a picture. Some unions are prearranged, or fated with a spell, or there are notable gaps in the story during which time these girls and their suitors presumably fall in love. But how does this happen, the falling part, the plunge? Can we trace the way a love-bond begins to form, and if so, can we study its reversal, the way a love-bond begins to break?

Let P^1 = my Parents on their first date. Let 1964 be the Year of our Lord—a nation in mourning for its young president, a Prince Charming who loved more women than he married. His beautiful widow begins her katabasis with two small children in tow. Their forest now in Technicolor, their future fuzzy in the crystal ball.

My mother has seen my father already. She has seen him in 1963 ascending the Sears Roebuck & Co. escalator stairs. He is tall and lean and handsome, dressed in a dark suit and headed for a young manager's training meeting. She tells the woman she works with, selling shoes for small commissions: "That's the man I'm going to marry someday."

Later, they collide in a stairwell, and he offers her a ride home. She tells me, "Never climb into a strange man's car. He could have chloroformed me, put a gun to my head, dropped me into the sea."

My mother is no believer in love or fate. She is no disciple of happy ever after.

My father is busy with the holidays, relatives visiting from out of town. Their paths fail to cross. Perhaps they will not become star-crossed lovers after all.

"Nice girls wait by the phone," she says, "but they never place the call."

Then, it is spring, and the cherry blossoms are dripping their sweetness onto University Boulevard. It may (or may not) be significant that this is a leap year. My future father finds my future mother in the shoe department (a Cinderella story—*almost, not quite*), and he says, "Would you like to play tennis with me?" It is a real invitation, an authentic date. She pretends to check a calendar, which is really a notebook of old grocery lists.

My mother's mother, watching her daughter iron the white tennis skirt and light knit sweater, instructs, "Make sure to let him win."

My mother, hovering over my desk: "Never let him win. Never let him think he can defeat you."

They tell the story differently. In each account, the teller is triumphant. After my father wins, or after my mother wins, they both agree they went out for Chinese food. I picture them sitting on the cold vinyl booths at Yen Wor Village, chow mein and tiger prawns steaming on a platter between them. The hot mustard makes my father sneeze; my mother says "Bless you" and means it.

If no points are scored in a tennis match, the result is called "love." (Let 0 = Love. Let 0–0 = Love-Love.) Perhaps it should be called "unrequited love." I make a note of this in my journal: *Love is an outcome where no one wins.*

We are reading *Hamlet* now. I am thinking of my mother and my father and of Ophelia, of how much I want not to end up as any of them.

Across the hall, Mr. Nowak writes in his blocky man-print: *FOUR STANDARDS NECESSARY FOR ELEMENTS TO BE USEFUL IN RADIOMETRIC DATING.*

Soon, his hand is tired. He passes out a ditto instead.

I. THE NUMBER OF PARENT ATOMS AND DAUGHTER ATOMS MUST BE MEASURABLE.

Let P^2 = my parents, who outnumber me two to one. There should have been more of me, I am reminded ($I > 1$), like an onion-skinned series of paper dolls unfolded longways across a dining room table.

"Remember you're our only daughter," my mother sighs. "And the man you marry will be our only son-in-law."

At the all-girls school, we have no boys to ask us to the dance. I am a nice girl who waits by a white shell phone on a wicker nightstand, knowing no one will call. "It's a tolo, Mother," I explain. "It means the girl *has* to ask the boy."

My mother is no believer in love or fate, but strategy she reveres. Strategy is sacred.

"Life is a tolo," my mother says. "The girl *always* chooses the boy, but the good girl makes him believe he chose her."

"What if the feeling is mutual? Couldn't they choose each other?"

She laughs now, her lips red as a boutonnière. "Don't be silly. Someone always wants the other more."

"If that's true, then isn't one person always a little desperate, and the other always a little disappointed?"

My mother is no disciple of happy ever after. "Better to be disappointed than desperate," she says, tipping her hands like scales. "There's no such thing as a perfect match."

In other words, *Love is an outcome where no one wins.*

II. THE PARENT ELEMENT MUST DECAY RAPIDLY ENOUGH TO PRODUCE MEASURABLE AMOUNTS OF THE DAUGHTER ELEMENT, BUT MEASURABLE AMOUNTS OF THE PARENT ELEMENT MUST ALSO BE PRESENT IN THE SAMPLE.

Let $P^2 + MA =$ my parents in middle age. My mother complains about my father's paunch, the way his body has changed for the worse since they married. "Think of J. R. Ewing on *Dallas,*" she cries, "then look at Larry Hagman now."

My father knows better than to comment on my mother's body. He keeps a calendar of women in assorted bikinis, their bellies tight and smooth, each navel a single, winking eye.

"So, your mother says you need a date to the dance." I look up from my father's overstuffed chair, a place I have taken to reading. I look past the women on the wall—a flesh-baring chorus of them, a strange congregation—to where he sits, bent over his desk with a straightedge, his graph paper with soft green lines.

"Not necessarily. It's just a dance. It isn't really that important."

"But these are the good years," my father says, turning to face me. "You want to get out there, mix with people, get a sense of what your prospects are."

"Or what?"

"What?" His head swivels back over his shoulder.

"What's the alternative? If I never went to a single dance, what would happen to me?" Juliet, after all, had gone dancing, and still she wound up dead. Ophelia, who attended the theater, drowned herself in shallow water.

"Well, I'm afraid," my father says, removing his glasses and rubbing his eyes. "I'm afraid you might end up a wallflower—like my sister."

In other words, *No one can pick a flower unless she blooms in plain sight.*

When Aunt Linda and I walk along the rocky shore, we often recite from poems we have read, which is easier than sharing poems we have written.

"Do you know this one? *When old age shall this generation waste, / Thou shalt remain, in midst of other woe / Than ours, a friend to man, to whom thou say'st, / 'Beauty is truth, truth beauty'—that is all / Ye know on earth, and all ye need to know.*"

"John Keats," she says. "He died young."

"He was twenty-five and had a really bad fever. But at least people remember him."

Aunt Linda stoops to study a piece of beach glass, smooth as a wafer and bluer than anyone's eyes. "What do you mean, 'At least people remember him'?"

"It seems like when women die, they're completely forgotten. Unless they're really, really beautiful. Then—only then—do they leave a lasting impression."

She lifts the glass, considers its weight, its beauty, then leaves it behind. "Who are you thinking of?"

"Ophelia mostly. Hamlet dumps her, and then she dies offstage. They make a big show of how much they cared about her at the funeral, but after that, no one ever mentions her again."

We wander on a while longer in silence, the Alki lighthouse coming slowly into view. "I guess I always assumed Ophelia *was* really, really beautiful," she says. "There are so many paintings of her."

"Did you date much in high school?" I ask, the question like a sudden gust of wind.

The zipper of her parka comes all the way to her chin, so Aunt Linda's mouth has a habit of hiding behind it. She seems to consider my question like the beach glass. Then: "Do you know this one? *For the sword outwears its sheath, / And the soul outwears the breast, / And the heart must pause to breathe, / And love itself have rest.*"

"Lord Byron. It was on my test. But—" I lay my hand on her crinkly sleeve. "Do you think that's the way it always is, what the poem describes? Because if love always wears out, then why would people ever pursue it?"

She doesn't look at me as she says it. She stares out across the still, gray waters of Puget Sound, bleak and beautiful at the same time. "Think of all the stories you know. The endings never change, but that doesn't stop you from reading them."

In other words, *The Troll is always under the bridge. The Wolf is always waiting in the woods.*

"And a lot worthwhile can happen in a story," I reason, "before you reach the end."

I can tell from her eyes that Aunt Linda is smiling at me, a kind of wistful smile like she thinks me foolish and admirable at the same time.

"What? What is it?"

"You just—sometimes you remind me of your father."

III. LITTLE OR NO DAUGHTER ELEMENT MUST HAVE BEEN PRESENT IN THE SAMPLE WHEN IT WAS FORMED.

Let 0 = Love. Let O = Ophelia. We use the zero in math to indicate the absence of something. We use Ophelia, marked by a letter resembling zero, to indicate the absence of something, too. Both mark an outcome where no one wins.

"Did you ever wonder who I would be?" I ask my mother. "How did you even know you wanted to have me?"

"What kind of question is that?" (Let Q be the most persistent question.) She is making her bed, a long ordeal of pillows arranged in a particular way. It is my parents' bed, but like everything else in their room, the female pronoun presides. (*Her* bureau. *Her* closet. *Her* chaise lounge.)

My father is a guest in this room. Sometimes he seems a guest in this life.

"We weren't having *you*," my mother says. "We were having a baby, which is a lot like having a lump of dough. You have to shape it, knead it, give it a reason to rise. Wonder has nothing to do with it."

"So—I'm like bread to you?"

She props a porcelain doll against the pillow shaped like a tootsie roll. "Yes, I guess. You're bread." My mother tosses her hands in the air. "For better or worse, you are the bread we made."

I think I seem a little desperate now. I think she seems a little disappointed.

Let S = Strategy, which is sacred. My parents take me with them to the Ericksons' house. It is game night, the adult couples arranged around card tables eating mixed nuts and drinking wine from large, refrigerator boxes. I used to stay with my grandmother on nights like these; now I have grown accustomed to staying home alone.

"Why am I going with you again?"

"Stop pestering me about it," my mother snaps, primping in the passenger-side mirror. "And here"—she hands me a small vial of *eau de toilette*—"daub some of this behind your ears."

MaryAnne Erickson greets us at the door, a large woman with a round, pink face animate as a cartoon character. "Julie, it's so lovely to see you!" she exclaims, even as I have just seen her at church the previous Sunday. "Come in! Come in!" She wraps her plush arm around my shoulder and ushers me inside. "Everyone, Julie is here." The other couples wave and smile.

Am I mistaken, or is there something conspiratorial in their faces? Am I an unsuspecting hostage, as Mrs. Erickson guides me away from the crowd and into the kitchen?

"So," she grins, "tell me how things are going for you at your high school."

"As well as can be expected," I say. I have grown practiced in the art of being vague.

"I'm glad to hear it." She clasps her hands, then gestures to the small table in the breakfast nook. "Sit down. Let me get you a Coke. Would you like a cherry in it?"

I nod and interlace my fingers in my lap, the way I sit in mass, so quiet and prim as to become incontestable—invisible even.

"Your mom tells me you're quite the swimmer," she says, pouring the fizzy beverage into a glass. "I think that's fantastic. I was a swimmer myself," and she winks at me, "in my day."

I study Mrs. Erickson now at the counter, her wide hips, her large, drooping breasts, her rhododendron body. I realize that she is pretty, inviting, the way they never tell you larger women are. And yet, she had been a swimmer. I knew well the expectations of the cutlass body, the surfboard body, depending on the stroke you swam.

"The thing about swimming is that it keeps you in great shape, but if you ever stop doing it, watch out! The calories will catch up with you."

Now her son Karl appears in the doorway. He is tall and razor-thin, his body long and clamped as a mussel shell. "Speak of the devil! Now here is someone who can never get enough calories, can you, darling? He eats like a horse, and there's still not enough meat on those bones."

Karl blushes, says nothing. "Julie, you remember Karl, don't you?"

"Yes—from middle school and church." I see him every weekend, so he is hard to forget, yet like me, straddling the line between visible and not.

Karl sets about fixing himself a sandwich, not looking at me and dodging his mother's eyes.

"I thought this might be a good time for you two to get re-acquainted. Karl goes to Seattle Lutheran now, and he's a swimmer, too."

"That's nice," I smile. I can see where this is going. Karl has no interest in me. I'm the plain girl sipping a Coke at his kitchen table. He's the plain boy eating salami and sourdough over the kitchen sink.

"Maybe you'd like to offer our guest something to eat?" Mrs. Erickson prods.

"Oh, I'm fine," I say. "I'm full." This is what my mother says nice girls always say, even if they're starving.

I am starting to see the world in plays, the moments in scenes. Perhaps Karl is the Hamlet of this performance, his mother Gertrude, the one who would truly mourn me if I died. It is becoming clear to me that I have been cast as a stranger in my own story, more times than not. *Xenogenesis* (X), the word I learned in last year's biology class. Let X = production of offspring entirely different from either parent. Let X = I.

When Karl steps off-stage again, his mother—embarrassed, apologetic—sits down with me at the table, says, "I've watched you grow up, Julie, and I think the future has stunning things in store."

I have not been the best daughter. The word *misfit* comes to mind. Not only "strange, freakish," but literally—"the wrong fit." I have never felt at home in my own body, which was handed down to me—made for me—by my parents. (The dough they kneaded, the daughter they needed . . .)

Still I can see, as MaryAnne takes my hands in hers, smiling at me and telling me what a nice girl I am, how full of potential, that I would be—as Ophelia would have been—an extraordinary daughter-in-law.

IV. THE SAMPLE USED MUST HAVE BEEN CHEMICALLY ISOLATED FROM OUTSIDE CHEMICAL CHANGES.

Let Date (D_1) = the day of the month or year as specified by a given number. In this case, let D_1 = the autumn tolo, my school's version of a homecoming dance. Let Date (D_3) = a romantic rendezvous arranged in advance at an appointed place and time. In this case, let D_3 = my first date with Karl Erickson, with whom I have never held a conversation.

Let Date (D_2) = a sweet, dark brown, oval fruit containing a hard stone. In this case, since I have never tasted this fruit, let D_2 = a metaphor. Even something as desirable as romance—as being seen in public being desired, pantomiming desire in return—contains a hard stone of truth. The truth is not always beautiful.

Let all the letters (D_{1-3}) be multivalent, just as they always are.

My parents drive me to the Ericksons' house, since neither Karl nor I can drive. I wear a white dress without sleeves that shows my shoulders. They are not as lovely as Olivia Hussey's shoulders; they are firm and tan and broad. Someone perhaps could find them beautiful, but that someone is not Karl Erickson, who stands fidgeting with his tie in the living room light.

I look up at the window, at my date awash in sallow fluorescence, and I think no one should bother to cut him out in little stars. His body a matchstick in a too-big suit, the flame tip his dark, over-gelled hair. I think, *Karl Erickson could never be heaven to me,* but there is no malice in it. I see clearly that this is no one's fault.

We exchange flowers in plastic cases. Mine is a wrist corsage that requires no assistance from anyone. I wear it all night like a cumbersome watch. Karl's father pins the boutonnière to his lapel.

"Oh, Jim, I remember being that young!" Mrs. Erickson exclaims. "We have to take a picture, for posterity." When things age, we call them dated. All my parents' photographs have a yellow tinge. Dating is a record of aging, and we are on the record now, shoulder to shoulder, two statues positioned in front of a hearth.

If this dance were a tennis match, I would say we were missing, conspicuously, both rackets and a viable net. There is such palpable absence—of interest, of attraction, of *chemistry.* We are not a good match, and the feeling is mutual. All night I clutch my little clutch bag. All night Karl looks over my shoulder as we dance, imagining he is somewhere else. Perhaps imagining he is someone else, or I am, or both.

Mr. Nowak is there, our chaperone, teacher of the relationship science. I try to avoid his eyes, but now, this time, he sees me and is visibly surprised.

"Julie?" He wants to make the exclamation point sound, but his inflection suggests a question instead. "You're here?"

"I am."

"And who's your date?"

"Oh, this is—Karl Erickson. He's—" and I find I have no adjectives to describe him. He occupies no space in my mind. "—a swimmer," I say at last.

"Well, welcome. Have some punch."

Since the dance is held at the aquarium, we are surrounded by large tanks of underwater creatures. This is a calming fact somehow. We sit side by side on the carpeted stairs of the observation room, gazing through the misty blue water at the fish. I have been watching the other couples, too, trying to discern which ones are really in love, or falling.

Sarah Korkowski, the math teacher's daughter, wears a black velvet blouse and a rainbow skirt that stretches out like a parachute. When she spins around, it opens, and I find my eyes drawn to the length of her legs, their long, taut beauty. Her date is just a shadow to me; he never comes fully into focus. And Anna Shope, who kisses her date full on the mouth as they sway in time to the music—she seems to have blood bating in her cheeks, and the blood rises in mine as I watch her. Karl has not said a word to me all night.

"So, what do you want to do—after this?"

"Go home," he says, not looking at me.

"No. I mean—after high school—*with your life.*"

"College."

"Any particular field of study?"

"Accounting."

"Then what?"

"Be an accountant, I guess." He takes my cup without asking and returns with more punch.

Now I'm feeling playful, like I have nothing to lose. "Why did your parents name you Karl?"

"What?" A glance in my direction.

"Your name—what does it mean?"

He sighs, bored and with nowhere to go. His knee keeps bobbing up and down in his pleated dress slacks. "A free man, I think."

I laugh a little, but he doesn't ask why.

"Well, my parents were going to name me Juliet," I lie. Another predictable silence. "But then, after they had me, they changed their minds."

Even if he had looked at me, I still would have disappeared.

6. THE BODY IS A LOCKET.

This time, let P = Prolepsis, for we are moving forward, flashing. First, all they wanted was to find me a date. Now all their talk is of waiting.

"The boys at college will want only One Thing (OT)—and you must never give it to them," my mother warns. I sit on my suitcase as she tugs the zipper around. "Think of your body as a brand-new car. You must always remember to lock it."

Our metaphors are growing muddled. Once I was soft as fresh-baked bread. Now I am hard as steel, as an automobile. My paint job must be perfect ("always look your best!"), but no one must be able to pry his way inside. ("Love is best served," my father quips, "by a good set of anti-lock brakes.")

In eighteen years, all my lessons have amounted to only One Thing (OT_2)—that, as a woman, withholding is my only real power.

With no aptitude for advanced math, I decide to become a philosopher. I will turn all mind, leave my body behind in a well-lit parking lot, the alarm system mobilized.

All my love affairs will be with dead Greek men. No sex, only excessive stimulation of the cerebral cortex. The one of them I like best—Plotinus—writes, "To this end, you must set free your soul from all outward things and turn wholly within yourself." *Had I not done this already? Was this not called Adolescence?*

I have come so far, I think, from the mansion of a love I once longed to possess. (*Let C = Celibacy, let c = chosen.*) I grow ascetic in my pursuits, finicky with food, attracted to isolation. Some nights I climb out of bed and force myself to sleep on the floor.

My roommate is a blond, lithe girl—a swimmer with a swimmer's body. I try not to notice her, the way she is so much of this world, predisposed to warmth and affection. "Do you listen to Jewel?" she asks.

"Who?" I am presently tunneling through a book on apophatic theology.

"OK. I'm going to pretend you did *not* just ask me that. Jewel! *Hello!*" Becky flashes me a picture of a woman who bears a striking resemblance to herself. "This is the new album, *Spirit,* but I have the old album, too, *Pieces of You.* Wanna hear it?"

I nod absently. I am too concerned with the *via negativa* for this intrusion from the real world. "Hey, she quotes that guy you like."

"What guy?"

"Plot-in-us?"

"Plo-TINE-us," I repeat, leaping up from my chair and wresting the CD from her hands. "*We are not separate from spirit; we are in it.*"

"Cool," Becky grins. "Let's listen."

If Juliet was a poet, was Jewel a philosopher? "I think she's more of a hippie," Becky chimes from the other room.

"But she is an itinerant, right, traveling around in her van?" Many philosophers prefer this lifestyle.

"OK, Miss Big Words. Whatever you say."

I have been listening to the first song on the *Spirit* album compulsively for three days. "I've never heard any music like this," I say. "What do you call it?"

"Folk, I guess. What do you usually listen to?"

"What my parents like—Benny Goodman and the Big Band era."

"The what?" Becky approaches me and wraps her arms around my neck. "That just seems to warrant a hug."

I notice that whenever Becky touches me, all the golden hairs on my arms prickle and rise. Her physical presence has the same effect as a great idea or a stellar word play. But there are other effects, too: quickening pulse, sudden sweats, a queasy, seasick feeling like the floor beneath me has moved.

And now there is Jewel, another name that could have been mine but isn't, a voice that seems to call out through the lyrics, addressing itself to me: *You try to find yourself / in the abstractions of religion.* (It's true! I have!) In the abstractions of love, too—the idea of it, untested, unembodied. (Juliet again: *O, I have bought the mansion of a love, but not possess'd it!*)

"Do you think Jewel is a virgin?" I ask.

At this, Becky clicks on her light and gapes at me across the room. "What in the world are you thinking? She's like thirty years old! Of course she's not a virgin."

"Well, my Aunt Linda is, and she's like fifty years old."

At this, Becky frowns. "Is she a nun or something?"

"Not exactly. She just—I guess she just loves Jesus very, very much."

"I don't get that," Becky sighs. "Wasn't Jesus all about feeding the hungry, helping the sick? Why would he want people to deprive themselves?"

Let P = Prolepsis, again.

I switch from philosophy to a psychology major. This seems the difference to me between introspection and interspection, the difference, more precisely, between dropping down the well of my own loneliness versus studying the cultural affliction of loneliness itself. Psychology was a "soft" science, a "social" science, predicated more on patterns than on proof. In other words, it was more the poetic than the mathematical imperative. (Let P = the set {Prolepsis, Poiesis, Pattern, et al.})

Before long, I am also an English major.

Becky has gone to study abroad, but she has left her Jewel CDs with me. Now I try to ask myself what Jewel would do, instead of the more familiar variation. I have begun to unlock my body consciously, door by door, to leave the dome light on. But it is not exactly as I had expected—not quite *succumbing*, not quite *rebelling*. I discover it is possible to kiss back, even deeply, my tongue softening like a plum inside another's mouth, and yet, when it is over, and even as it is still occurring, I sense this separateness—my spirit from my body, my spirit from his body, too.

Ben fears his own body just as I fear mine—all our inherent limitations and untested capacities. Together we pore over a poem from literature class, a poem by Robert Hass titled "A Story About the Body."

In this story-poem, a composer and a painter working one summer at an artist colony find themselves drawn to each other. One evening, the painter, sensing the composer's desire for her and explaining that her desire for him is mutual, reveals that she has had a double mastectomy. Once he knows her breasts are missing, her dreamed-of body incomplete, the composer declines to make love with her, saying, "I'm sorry. I don't think I could." When he wakes the next day, she has left a blue bowl full of rose petals and dead bees on his doorstep.

"It doesn't look like a poem," Ben says, a bit suspicious. "And it's already called a *story,* so why isn't it published as fiction?"

"I think a story can be a poem," I reply, but this is tentative. I am testing a hypothesis.

"And what makes this a stanza and not a paragraph?"

"Maybe it can be both," I say. (↔)

Ben is thin to the point of being frail. All the veins are visible in his arms, and his fingers are nimble, always in motion. "I play piano," he reveals to me. "I read music, and I also write my own."

The professor wants us to consider the poem symbolically. *Was there any other way to think about things?* "What do the rose petals represent? What about the dead bees?"

⧗

This poem becomes our excuse for extended conversation. "You compose," I prod over dinner in the University Commons. "Explain the young composer's motivations to me."

"Well, we're not all the same. That's like saying, because you're a woman, you should know why the painter leaves that bowl on his doorstep."

"But I *do* know why," I tell Ben proudly, "and it isn't because I'm a woman either. It's because I'm a psychology major."

"I thought you were an English major."

"I am that, too." (↔)

"So, why?" We are both self-conscious about eating in front of each other, embarrassed that our bodies have such needs at all.

"The bowl is a mirror of his perception of her. She is holding the mirror up for him, a very Lacanian move"—I say this, even as I am still a bit fuzzy on Lacan. "The contents of the bowl are the layers of his perception. First, he thought she was a flower, the most beautiful flower in the world—a rose. Even though I think, personally, the iris is a much more beautiful and interesting flower, this is about archetypes and Carl Jung." I am a bit fuzzy on Jung as well. "So the rose petals stand for beauty, and the dead bees are the death of his desire for her—like birds and bees—like *sex,*" I whisper, "after he finds out that her body isn't what he thought it was."

Ben nods, turning his fork in circles like a compass. "OK. So why does she say, 'I think you would like to have me,' like she's a piece of jewelry or a snow globe or something—like she is something he could take home with him in his pocket."

"Well, because that's how it feels sometimes."

"How what feels?"

"Being a girl, being *female*—you feel like you can only offer yourself or refuse. Like you can *be had* or *not be had* but can never actually *have.*"

"Is there a word for that, in psychology?" His eyes are too large for their small sockets, owlish, sad, and kind.

A caesura, during which my fork also turns in circles. "Not that I'm aware of."

We stare at each other a long time, leaning forward until we become like the two faces in Rubin's figure-ground illusion. (*Almost, not quite.*)

"So, why do you think the bowl is blue?" Ben asks at last.

I swallow the nothing that is filling up my mouth. (Let 0 = Love). "Maybe it's the color of his eyes?"

Let P = Prolepsis, once more.

Ten years in the future, I will spread my legs for a stranger in a white coat, press my feet into the stirrups, and close my eyes. The doctor studies my chart in silence, reviews my answers to the questions her nurse has asked me. I know this procedure now and no longer startle as the cold metal slides inside me, as the cold air rushes in behind. Instead, it is her words—the first words she has ever spoken to me—that take me by surprise: "Were you ever heterosexual?" the doctor inquires. Overhead, the fluorescent light is buzzing, as though it were full of bees. I look around to be sure, but there are no flowers in this small, sterile room.

"Excuse me?"

"It says in your chart that you have a female partner, but do you have a sexual history with men as well?"

"Yes," I stammer. "I have been with men, but I'm not sure—"

"*Bisexual* then." (↔) She says it conclusively and makes a note in my file.

Now the doctor withdraws the speculum and enters me with two fingers of her gloved hand. I wince and look away, thinking *how strange,* how the same action that has given rise to such pleasure—my lover pressing the long stem of her body against me, my curved ribs rising to meet hers—here, out of context, leaves me mute, embarrassed, numb.

"I'm not sure I'm bisexual," I say.

"But your history is. That's all I'm interested in. As a woman, if you have had sexual intercourse with a man, even once, you are at higher risk for the human papillomavirus than a woman who has never had sex with a man."

In the distance, a car alarm—its low, persistent wail.

"Overall, though, the risk must be much lower for women in lesbian relationships?" Sitting up now, squeezing the tissue paper tight between my thighs.

"Only if both women have no history of sexual contact with men, or with any other women who have had sexual contact with men." Her tone is matter-of-fact, verging toward irritation. She glides away from me on the low, wheeled stool.

"Well," I say, determined to claim the last word, "it wasn't a gold star I was seeking."

Let A = Analepsis, by way of afterword.

We have been on a date—Ben in a borrowed suit driving a borrowed car, me in a new dress from the clearance rack at The Bon Marche. We have been to a concert, live jazz by candlelight; the dessert and the check split between us.

I wish I could say to him what the woman in the story-poem says: "I think you would like to have me. I would like that too." But the truth is, I don't know how to say what I want, or how to name where my outer limits are. (*Let VN = Via Negativa,* a way of describing something by stating what it is not). I only know that I don't want for the night to end too soon.

Ben parks the car under a street lamp on University Boulevard. A late autumn rain smears Christmas lights like watercolors against the glass. He turns to me sweetly and says, "Should we wait this out?" When I nod, he leaps into the storm and opens the door to the back seat so we can sit close to each other, shivering for all sorts of reasons, and finally, without the emergency brake between us.

"Did you ever see the movie version of *Romeo and Juliet*—the old one, by Zeffirelli?" It is only half stalling. I really want to know.

"I think so—a long time ago. Why?"

"Well, there's this strange backstory to it. Remember how Olivia Hussey, the girl who plays Juliet, has a topless scene?"

"Oh, I remember that," Ben says, then blushes.

"So, she was fifteen at the time, and they had to get special permission to show her breasts, but later, when the movie came out, she wasn't allowed to see it in theaters because she wasn't eighteen. The age restriction was due to the nudity, but—"

"—she was the one who was nude!" Ben exclaims. "They wouldn't let her see her own self naked." We both laugh together, softly.

"Isn't that crazy? Lacan would have a field day."

"What would he say?" We are toying with each other's buttons, and our lips are very close to touching.

"I guess I don't really know, to be honest."

Then, we are kissing with our coats on, our fingers lacing and unlacing, our mouths by turn timid and urgent and breathless and quiet. "That's OK," he assures me. "I don't really know either."

7. ALL GAZING IS NAVEL GAZING.

Let M_n = the new millennium. Let M_n^2 = the new myopia. Era of status updates and reality television, of cell phones glowing with under-table texts.

In the midst of this, which, as a child, I heard differently—as *in the mist of this,* the moist confusion of the moment, the wet fog—I am eager for anachronism, an old-fashioned love story.

Let M_0 = the man who proposes to me, on bended knee, in my first grown-up apartment. I am taken with him, have been taken by him, my body pliant and eager to please. When he brings me garters and black lace stockings, I don them readily. I embrace the meta-need: wanting to be wanted (W^W), loving to be loved (L^L).

But there is one restriction I impose—no filming us. Likewise, no posing for photographs or performing before mirrors. "Why?" he presses, resting the camera on the windowsill. "Don't you want a record of this?"

"I'll write you a poem," I say.

"But—"

"It will be a vivid, image-centered poem," I promise, smiling.

"But—"

"I mean it. I don't want to see my body that way."

My fiancé believes further study has had the effect of brainwashing me. "And yes, I've heard of Laura Mulvey before," he sulks. "But I don't see what some feminist's theories of cinema have to do with our sex life."

"This isn't about Laura Mulvey," I say. "I shouldn't have used the word *gaze.*"

"Then, what is it about? Are you disgusted, ashamed? Is this your inner Puritan coming out after all?"

"No." He stands in the doorway, tall and broad-shouldered, his body blocking the light.

"Is it me? You don't want proof that you did these things with me?" (*Let W be the wounded twinge of his tone.*)

"No." For all the fables of joining hands and hearts, of lovers' bodies becoming one, I knew we were separate, our desires, too. This wasn't a failure but a fact.

"Everything I want or don't want is not a comment on you!"

From the scowl on his face, I might have said: *Love is an outcome where no one wins.*

As it turns out, there is more math in psychology than I had first realized. Let C = Covariance, meaning the measure of how two random variables change together. Let L = Love, another measure of how two random variables change together. (Let C = L.) In statistics and probability theory, if variables tend to show similar behavior, the covariance is a positive number. If they tend to show divergent behavior, the covariance is negative.

Let A_1 = Algorithm. *Algorithms for calculating variance play a major role in statistical computing. A key problem in the design of good algorithms is that formulas for the vari-*

ance may involve sums of squares, which can lead to numerical instability as well as to arithmetic overflow when dealing with large values.

Let A_2 = Aphorism. *Opposites attract, but birds of a feather stick together. Absence makes the heart grow fonder, but familiarity breeds contempt. Love him or leave him.*

What is the relationship between A_1 and A_2?

February 2002. We are trudging up the hill from the cinema where we have just seen an old-fashioned film in the style of Alfred Hitchcock. There is snow on the ground, and snow in the air—a clean cold like the night is made of glass, and we are inside it, tiny figures in a snow globe.

He has a habit of cinching my wrist instead of holding my hand. I have a habit of watching the moon instead of meeting his eyes.

Let M_1 = the Marriage. "We should start talking about it," he says. "June will be here before you know it." *Alt. Matrimony, Wedlock. A union between two persons designed to create kinship. A legal contract that establishes a household under the law. A joining of a man and woman into one flesh before God. A syzygy. A cleaving.*

Let M_2 = the MacGuffin. "Yes," I answer absently. *A plot device, or highly desired goal, that exists merely to drive the narrative forward, with little or no explanation as to why it is so important.* "Or we could just live together. Or—" *It is typically the central focus of the first act, and may come into play again at the climax, but sometimes it is actually forgotten by the end of the story.*

What is the relationship between M_1 and M_2?

Across the road in the Birnam Wood Apartments, a face alights in a window. Her eyes are downcast; she does not return my gaze. Something startles in my heart, like birds in the hedges, battering their wings. The magnitude of the covariance is not easy to interpret at this point (A_1). *Is it love at first sight?* (A_2) Later this night, I will use my lover's body as a ladder, trying to reach her—that light in the distance, apogee and zenith.

Let S = the Subjunctive. Let us suppose that I am willing to break my promise, to forego the dress and the ring and the blessing, the appointed hour in the orchard. Let us suppose I am willing to descend the dangerous night-trellis of *If*. To pass through the winter garden of *If and Only If*.

The words for this—*lovestruck, moonstruck, katabasis*.

The symbols—*iff*, ↔.

We are entering the realm of complex numbers (CN). *Complex numbers allow for solutions to certain equations that have no real solution.* (An illusion? A sleight of hand?) *They are indicated by the numerical phrase,* a + bi, *where a and b are real numbers and* i *is the imaginary unit.*

Where once we were two, now we are three, and I am leaning, all hypotenuse, the ladder against the house, the woman at the window. *But, soft! What light through yonder window breaks? It is the east, and Juliet is the sun.*

For the first time, I was not outside myself, looking in. I was not watching as someone else enacted desire upon me. *Covariance? Syzygy?*

Later: "It's hard to explain. I was present in a different way." A new radiance I carried around in my belly and chest cavity—like music.

The song in the background, looping: *I want somebody who sees me.*

The woman on the talk show, crying: *I spent too much time looking at myself through his eyes.*

The man in the house, leaving: *That isn't love; that's narcissism. You're two women. You only want to see yourselves.*

If you have traveled the requisite distance . . . *if* you have crossed the bridge and considered the Troll and passed through the woods and eluded the Wolf and blown a kiss homeward (for you won't go back) to your mother and your father . . . *then,* the road narrows again, slender as a fishbone.

If → *then.* Now commences your anabasis, the ultimate ascent.

In logic and related fields such as mathematics and philosophy, *iff* is a biconditional logical connective between statements. It is an abbreviation for *if and only if,* indicating that one statement is both necessary and sufficient for the other. The result is that the truth of either one of the connected statements requires the truth of the other.

Consider these conditions:

B is sufficient for L
L is necessary for B
¬*L is sufficient for* ¬*B*
¬*B is necessary for* ¬*L*

In this statement, *B* → *L,* where *B* is "each body is imperfect, separate, and real" and *L* is "both lovers rejoice in the presence of their lover's body." The following are four equivalent ways of expressing this relationship:

If both bodies are imperfect, separate, and real, then both lovers rejoice in the presence of their lover's body.

Only if the lovers rejoice in the presence of each other's bodies are their bodies imperfect, separate, and real.
If the lovers will not rejoice in the presence of each other's bodies, then their bodies are not imperfect, separate, and real.
Only if both bodies are not imperfect, separate, and real will the lovers not rejoice in the presence of each other's bodies.

We spread the red checkered picnic cloth on the grassy slope at the top of the mountain. It could be any place we have ever been, or any place we have yet to travel. We could be talking about Shakespeare, the way poems were written once versus the way they are written now.

I might say, "I think Shakespeare was not only a great poet, but also a philosopher, and a mathematician."

She might say, skeptical, "Philosopher, given, but what about the math?"

"Sonnets," I might reply, spreading mustard on a Kaiser roll, choosing from among the cold cuts and cheese. "I think a sonnet is another form of proof."

Or: we are lying together in a hammock splayed between the trees, when she might turn to me and say, her eyes blue as beach glass, "Do you remember anything about the new math? They tried to introduce it briefly at my school, but no one had even mastered the old math, so how could they master the new?"

Then, I might admit in a low voice, "I liked it better. I was interested in abstract concepts and grouping things together in sets. But we always came back, in the end, to the old way."

In the new mathematics, there must first be freedom of thought; second, we do not want to teach just words; and third, subjects should not be introduced without explaining the purpose or reason, or without giving any way in which the material could be really used to discover something interesting.

"And have you discovered anything interesting?" Her hand in my hand, our fingers laced.

Andre Breton once wrote, *I have discarded clarity as worthless. Working in darkness, I have discovered lightning.* (The tree trunk struck, then severed. Words for the image at last!)

"Maybe." I pass her my proof in fourteen lines:

You who are tacit to me now—in thought,
in deed, in every act of love tenderly
foreshadowed; how the heart, a slender knot
undone, permits this negative capacity;
what Keats has called "being in uncertainties . . .
mysteries," our disbeliefs suspended
in favor of some possible: those lilies
in full splendor, beneath the snow descended.
As when the bad luck comes and buries us
in cold, the season's long ellipsis hides
that sprig of green, this meadow's softness;
we shake our fists at the glib moon, the shrill tides.
See how we flower: your green truth, contemplative;
my own life's objective correlative.

Let FA = the Final Axiom: "Love opens in us a new set of eyes." We rejoice then in the presence of each other's bodies.

ACKNOWLEDGMENTS

Thank you to all the literary journal editors who first saw promise in this essay series!

SECTION I

This section, published as "Hourglass (I)," first appeared in *Blackbird,* Vol. 13, No. 1, Spring 2014, and was subsequently nominated for a 2014 Pushcart Prize.

The lines "*There is a time for the evening under starlight . . .*" are from T. S. Eliot's "East Coker," the second of his *Four Quartets,* first published in 1941. This long poem is my favorite from Eliot's body of work. As it turns out, it was Eliot's favorite from his own work, too.

SECTION II

This section, published as "Hourglass (II)," first appeared in *Blackbird,* Vol. 13, No. 1, Spring 2014.

SECTION III

This section, published as "Hourglass (III)," first appeared in *Southern Humanities Review,* Vol. 50, 1&2, 2016. In 2014, the essay was named a finalist for *The Fairy Tale Review* Essay Prize, and in 2017, it was listed as a "Notable Essay of 2016" in *Best American Essays 2017,* edited by Leslie Jamison.

The lines "*Ever just the same, / Ever a surprise*" belong to the song "Beauty and the Beast," written by lyricist Howard Ashman and composer Alan Menken for the Disney animated film *Beauty and the Beast,* 1991. The song was recorded by pop duet Celine Dion and Peabo Bryson and released later that year as the film's only single. You may have heard it at the roller rink, just as I did.

SECTION IV

This section, published as "Hourglass (IV)," first appeared in *Hunger Mountain,* Fall 2013, and later received a "Special Mention" in the 2013 *Pushcart Prize Anthology XXXIX.*

"Slim Waist Holds Sway in History" is a BBC news article originally published on January 10, 2007. You can read the article online here if you like: http://news.bbc.co.uk/2/hi/health/6247625.stm.

Robert Frost's "After Apple-Picking" was first published in *North of Boston,* his second poetry collection, in 1914.

"Prufrock" is a reference to the title speaker of T. S. Eliot's first professionally published poem, "The Love Song of J. Alfred Prufrock," which debuted in 1915 in the still-published-today *Poetry* magazine.

Denise Duhamel's "Spoon" was first published in *Ka-Ching!,* in 2009. I once heard Denise Duhamel read this poem at the 21C Hotel in Louisville, KY, which was the night of our auspicious first meeting, also in 2009.

Chris Abani's "Unholy Women" was first published in *Dog Woman* in 2004. We have never met in real life, but happily there is still time!

Sharon Olds's "The Death of Marilyn Monroe" was published in *The Dead and the Living* in 1983. It was the first collection of Olds's poetry I read, but far from the last. I have taught this poem in every iteration of my introductory, multi-genre creative writing course at Florida International University since 2012. In 2019, I met Sharon Olds for the first time at the Palm Beach Poetry Festival. Dream realized! The title of this book is intended as grateful homage to her life and work.

"Secrets of Marilyn Monroe's Hourglass Figure Revealed in Receipts" is a Celebrity News feature originally published on December 12, 2008, by *The Telegraph*. You can read the article online here if you like: https://www.telegraph.co.uk/news/celebritynews/3723964/Secrets-of-Marilyn-Monroes-hourglass-figure-revealed-in-receipts.html.

"The Catholic Tradition" is an unusual and extensive website, which brought back many memories from my years in Catholic school. The site's stated mission is as follows: "Reparation for Sin and Blasphemy, Prayers and Devotions, Catholic Truth and Catholic Classics Along with Commentary on the Signs of the Times, and Home Schooling Help for Catholic Homes and the Promotion of the Traditional Roman Rite, Which Every Catholic Has an Absolute Right To." I like the play on *rite/right* at the end. For more about Mary specifically from this site, you may wish to read here: http://www.catholictradition.org/Mary/beauty2.htm

The excerpt from Marilyn Monroe's unfinished letter to Joe DiMaggio comes from *Marilyn Monroe: The Biography*, by Donald Spoto, first published by Cooper Square Press in July 2001. I grew up in a home with no fewer than five biographies of Marilyn Monroe. I'm not sure if these books were ever read or if they were always intended to serve as part of our décor.

SECTION V

This section, published as "Hourglass (V)," first appeared in *The Seattle Review*, Vol. 6, No. 2, 2013.

The lines *"To turn woman is to turn / body"* are from the poem "Briseis" in Suzanne Paola's debut poetry collection,

Bardo, first published in 1998. I met Suzanne Paola when I became her student in Graduate Poetry Workshop during Winter Quarter 2002 at Western Washington University. She also directed my first poetry thesis.

The lines "*There is an alchemy in sorrow; it can be transmuted into wisdom*" are from Pearl S. Buck's 1950 memoir, *The Child Who Never Grew.* They were shared with me by my first creative writing teacher, Sally McLaughlin, at Holy Names Academy in 1997.

The lines "*I was a girl then, my chest its own walled garden*" are from the poem "The Leaving" in Brigit Pegeen Kelly's debut poetry collection, *In Place of Trumpets,* first published in 1988. I never had the chance to meet this poet in real life, but I suspect it would have been a lovely experience.

"A-Tisket A-Tasket" is a nursery rhyme first recorded in America in the late 1800s. It has a Roud Folk Song Index of 13188. My Grandma June was the first person ever to sing this song to me, sometime in the mid-1980s.

All quotes from William Shakespeare in this section come from *Romeo and Juliet,* a play that dates back to 1597. Like you, perhaps, this play was my first experience reading the Bard's work in a ninth-grade English class. *Romeo and Juliet* remained my favorite Shakespeare play until we read *The Tempest* senior year. When I saw *The Tempest* performed at the restored Globe Theatre in London in 2000 starring Vanessa Redgrave as Prospero, I knew it would be impossible thereafter to love any of Shakespeare's other plays more.

The lines "*When old age shall this generation waste, / Thou shalt remain, in midst of other woe / Than ours, a friend to man, to whom thou say'st, / 'Beauty is truth, truth beauty'—that is all / Ye know on earth, and all ye need to know*" comprise the final stanza of John Keats's famous ekphrastic poem, "Ode on a Grecian Urn," first published in 1819. Keats also famously wrote in his 1818 poem "Endymion"—"A thing of beauty is a joy forever." Throughout my childhood these words hung, unattributed, on a piece of stained glass in our living room window.

The lines "*For the sword outwears its sheath, / And the soul outwears the breast, / And the heart must pause to breathe, / And love itself have rest*" comprise the second stanza of George Gordon, Lord Byron's poem "So We'll Go No More a Roving," first published in 1830—though it was included in a letter to Thomas Moore in 1817. I first encountered this poem in British Literature with Sister Mary Annette when she asked me to read it aloud to the class.

The lines "*To this end, you must set free your soul from all outward things and turn wholly within yourself*" come from Plotinus's *The Six Enneads,* which were first compiled and edited by his student Porphyry circa 270 CE. I first encountered Plotinus my freshman year of college through an interdisciplinary seminar taught by a Classics professor and a Philosophy professor. This class was called "Community, Legacy, Identity, and Faith," and in it, I earned my first recorded transcript grade of B–. (How far I had fallen!) Shortly thereafter, I encountered Plotinus again on Jewel's 1998 studio album, *Spirit:* "*We are not separate from spirit; we are in it.*" If I could have earned a grade for my study of Jewel at that time, I am confident it would have been an A+.

The line "*You try to find yourself / in the abstractions of religion*" is from the song "Deep Water" on the *Spirit* album.

Robert Hass's prose poem "A Story About the Body" was published in *Human Wishes* in 1990. I know now that this collection was published the final week of my fourth-grade year, but I couldn't have imagined such a poem then. Later, after I had read the poem in college and discussed it at length with everyone I knew, I discovered the collection *Human Wishes* at a bookshop in Pike Place Market. The collection contains not only "A Story About the Body" but also another prose poem called "The Harbor at Seattle." When I read that poem for the first time, I was standing in the bookshop gazing out at the Seattle harbor, and I remember thinking, *This is what poems do, how they astonish us*. I have not yet met Robert Hass, but my fingers remain tightly crossed.

The lyric "*I want somebody who sees me*" comes from Dar Williams's song "As Cool as I Am," from her album *The Honesty Room,* released in 1996. In college, I wrote by hand—and gave my friend Ben the only copy—a screenplay based on this song. Sometimes I wish I still had that screenplay, though most days I prefer the memory of how lusciously terrible it was. Twenty years later, I still have the CD.

⧗

I love books, and I am grateful to all the people who have helped me love them throughout my life.

Thank you to my parents who read to me every night, and to all my teachers, who helped prepare me, even before I realized they were doing so, for a life of learning and teaching from books I love.

Thank you to all the authors who have written books I cherish and to all the authors who will go on to do so—among them, my extraordinary students at Florida International University.

Thank you to my colleagues who have written many of those books I cherish and who have mentored many of those students I cherish, too—Lynne Barrett, Richard Blanco, Cindy Chinelly, Debra Dean, Denise Duhamel, John Dufresne, Campbell McGrath, and Les Standiford. Much gratitude also to Térèse Campbell, Nick Garnett (and formerly Marina Pruna and Emily Jalloul), and Marta Lee, who make so much of what happens in our program possible.

Thank you to Johnny D. for always practicing the peripatetic method with me, as any true contemporary South Floridian philosophers would do!

Thank you to Denise Duhamel and Brenda Miller for deepening my love of books that much further by writing books with me!

Thank you especially to all my professors and peers in the doctoral Interdisciplinary Humanities program at the University of Louisville, where this project, *Just an Ordinary Woman*

Breathing, began to take shape in my mind—and without which courses and conversations I am certain the final version would not exist. (Annette Allen, Catherine Fosl, Paul Griner, and Brian Leung—think of this collection as my "shadow dissertation," started just as soon as the real one was ready to defend!)

Thank you to everyone at The Ohio State University Press who shepherded my manuscript from submission to print, especially my editor and fellow joyful fast-talker, Kristen Elias Rowley.

Thank you always to Dana Anderson, Tom Campbell, James Allen Hall, and Anna Rhodes, for more reasons than I can name here, or anywhere.

Thank you to my Outlaws-turned-Inlaws, Kim and Matt Striegel, who have always been family no matter what the law said; and to the Strieglets, who made me one lucky aunt—Evie, Nolan "Super Hondo," and Sam.

Thank you to Tybee and Tina, magnificent felines, who sit on all the books and shelves, all the notes and drafts, of everything I read and write. (And to Oliver, "Ollie" to all who knew him—the cattest of them all—in memoriam.)

Most of all, thank you to Angie Griffin—my favorite person, partner, and spouse; best reader I know; best librarian, too. How I love this life we've written together these nearly eighteen years!

21st CENTURY ESSAYS

David Lazar and Patrick Madden, Series Editors

This series from Mad Creek Books is a vehicle to discover, publish, and promote some of the most daring, ingenious, and artistic nonfiction. This is the first and only major series that announces its focus on the essay—a genre whose plasticity, timelessness, popularity, and centrality to nonfiction writing make it especially important in the field of nonfiction literature. In addition to publishing the most interesting and innovative books of essays by American writers, the series publishes extraordinary international essayists and reprint works by neglected or forgotten essayists, voices that deserve to be heard, revived, and reprised. The series is a major addition to the possibilities of contemporary literary nonfiction, focusing on that central, frequently chimerical, and invariably supple form: The Essay.

Just an Ordinary Woman Breathing
    Julie Marie Wade

My Private Lennon: Explorations from a Fan Who Never Screamed
    Sibbie O'Sullivan

On Our Way Home from the Revolution: Reflections on Ukraine
    Sonya Bilocerkowycz

Echo's Fugue
    Desirae Matherly

This One Will Hurt You
    Paul Crenshaw

The Trouble with Men: Reflections on Sex, Love, Marriage, Porn, and Power
    David Shields

Fear Icons: Essays
    Kisha Lewellyn Schlegel

Sustainability: A Love Story
    Nicole Walker

Hummingbirds Between the Pages
    Chris Arthur

Love's Long Line
Sophfronia Scott

The Real Life of the Parthenon
Patricia Vigderman

You, Me, and the Violence
Catherine Taylor

Curiouser and Curiouser: Essays
Nicholas Delbanco

Don't Come Back
Lina María Ferreira Cabeza-Vanegas

A Mother's Tale
Phillip Lopate